Introduction to
Online
Learning

A Guide for Students

Julie L. Globokar
Kaplan University

SSAGE

Los Angeles | London | New Delhi
Singapore | Washington DC

For information:

SAGE Publications, Inc.
2455 Teller Road
Thousand Oaks, California 91320
E-mail: order@sagepub.com

SAGE Publications India Pvt. Ltd.
B 1/I 1 Mohan Cooperative
 Industrial Area
Mathura Road, New Delhi 110 044
India

SAGE Publications Ltd.
1 Oliver's Yard
55 City Road
London EC1Y 1SP
United Kingdom

SAGE Publications Asia-Pacific
 Pte. Ltd.
33 Pekin Street #02-01
Far East Square
Singapore 048763

Printed in the United States of America

Library of Congress Cataloging-in-Publication Data

Globokar, Julie.
Introduction to online learning : a guide for students / Julie L. Globokar.
    p. cm.
Includes bibliographical references and index.
ISBN 978-1-4129-7822-4 (pbk.)

    1. Distance education—United States. 2. Educational technology—United States. 3. Web-based instruction. I. Title.

LB2328.15.U6G56 2010
371.35'8—dc22   2010003001

This book is printed on acid-free paper.

10   11   12   13   14   10 9   8   7   6   5   4   3   2   1

Acquisitions Editor:	Jerry Westby
Editorial Assistant:	Nichole O'Grady
Production Editor:	Libby Larson
Typesetter:	C&M Digitals (P) Ltd.
Proofreader:	Theresa Kay
Indexer:	Terri Corry
Cover Designer:	Arup Giri
Marketing Manager:	Stephanie Adams

Introduction to
Online
Learning

Contents

Preface   **ix**

Chapter 1: Debunking the Myths of Online Education   **1**

Introduction   1
Myth #1: Taking Online Courses Is "Settling"
   for a Lesser-Quality Education   2
Myth #2: I Am Feeling Overwhelmed;
   Online Learning Must Not Be for Me   3
Myth #3: I Don't Know My Way
   Around a Computer: I Can't Do This!   3
Myth #4: With Online Education, I Am "Going It Alone"   4
Myth #5: I Am Online All the Time: This Will Be Easy!   7
Myth #6: Online Learning Requires
   Less Time Than Traditional Education   8
Myth #7: Since This Is an Online Course, I Can Complete
   the Coursework Whenever I Want   9
Myth #8: My Online Coursework Will Not
   Be Respected by Others   11
Conclusion   12
Reflection Questions   12
Chapter Checklist   12
Related Resources   13

Chapter 2: Where Do I Start?   **15**

Introduction   15
Technology Basics   16
Getting Comfortable With the Online Campus   19
Exploring the Online Classroom   20
Knowing What to Look For   22
Conclusion   27

Reflection Questions   27
Chapter Checklist   28
Related Resources   28

Chapter 3: Getting Organized   **29**

Introduction   29
Getting Organized   30
Where to Find the Space   32
Special Considerations When Working at Home   35
Finding an Office in the Community   37
Where to Find the Time   38
The Importance of Balance   41
Conclusion   42
Reflection Questions   42
Chapter Checklist   43
Related Resources   43

Chapter 4: Where Do I Turn for Help?
Knowing Your Resources   **45**

Introduction   45
Getting Answers to School-Specific Questions   46
Technological Resources   47
Academic Resources   49
Social Resources   51
Counseling Services   52
Financial Support   54
Conclusion   57
Reflection Questions   57
Chapter Checklist   57
Related Resources   58

Chapter 5: When the Worst Happens and How to Cope   **61**

Introduction   61
The Importance of Perspective   61
Technology Matters   62
Tips and Tricks to Minimize Technical Catastrophes   63
Responding to Common Problems   65
Family, Work, or Personal Emergencies   68
Physical Limitations to Writing   69
School-Related Problems   70
When You Have Fallen Behind . . .   71

Conclusion   71
Reflection Questions   72
Chapter Checklist   72
Related Resources   72

Chapter 6: Learning Styles   **73**

Introduction   73
Know Your Strengths   73
The Delivery of Information   75
Kolb's Learning Styles   77
Other Considerations in Learning Style   80
Conclusion   80
Reflection Questions   81
Chapter Checklist   81
Related Resources   81

Chapter 7: Written Communication   **83**

Introduction   83
Computer-Mediated Communication, Academic Style   83
Discussion Boards   84
E-mails   91
Formal Writing Assignments   93
Conclusion   93
Reflection Questions   94
Chapter Checklist   94
Related Resources   94

Chapter 8: Conducting Quality Research for Your Online Class   **95**

Introduction   95
Why Research?   96
Types of Resources   97
Researching for Your Online Class   103
Conclusion   105
Reflection Questions   105
Chapter Checklist   105
Related Resources   106

Chapter 9: Citing Your Sources   **107**

Introduction   107
Citing 101   107
Knowing *When* to Cite   110

Knowing *How* to Cite   113
Preparing to Cite Your Sources   115
Conclusion   116
Reflection Questions   117
Chapter Checklist   117
Related Resources   118

Index   **119**

About the Author   **123**

Preface

Most people think of a "standard college experience" as one in which students move into the college dorms after high school graduation. They attend college orientation to learn about different campus resources. They study their campus map to find the bookstore and library. They stock up on notebooks, pens, and #2 pencils. They sit through a number of classes each week, sometimes engaging in vibrant academic discussions, sometimes listening attentively to instructors' lectures, and sometimes nodding off in the back row after a late night of studying. They go to the student union to study for quizzes and exams. They use the computer lab to type and print papers, which they hand in to their instructors on the due date.

Increasingly, the "standard college experience" is becoming less standard. Students are enrolling in courses that are taken, in whole or in part, over the Internet. The growth of online enrollments has far outpaced higher education more generally.[1] Some online students have the traditional "college life," living in the dorms but choosing to take some of their classes online for convenience. Others return to school under quite different circumstances, pursuing their educational goals after years in the workforce or military, or as a stay-at-home parent. This is an exciting time to be a college student; more institutions are offering courses online, where students with common educational goals can transcend geographic and social barriers to converge in a virtual space that enables them to benefit from the expertise of their instructors and the wealth of knowledge that comes from the diverse experiences of their classmates. The online classroom provides a space for personal growth, meaningful interactions, and quality instruction. The best part: You can partake in this educational revolution without leaving the comfort of your own home.

A number of engaging and insightful books are already available to help guide college students on their path to success; unfortunately,

Figure 0.1 Students Enrolled in at Least One Online Class, Millions

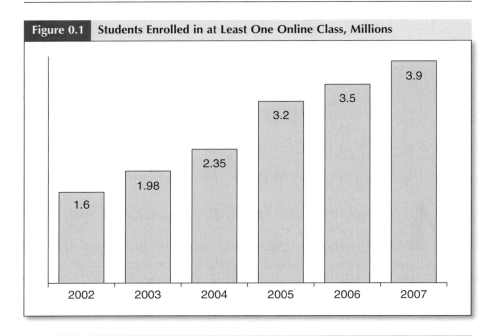

Source: Compiled with data from Sloan-C; http://www.sloan-c.org/publications/
freedownloads.asp[2]

most of these books are tailored to the old "standard" in college education. There are few resources available to help guide students through their transition to the online classroom. Online learning can be satisfying and rigorous, enjoyable and accommodating, but as with most things in life, success is more likely for those who know what to expect. It has been proposed that the process of becoming an "e-learner" actually involves five interrelated tasks:

1. Becoming familiar with relevant technologies

2. Navigating the classroom Web site

3. Learning the course content

4. Relying on self-motivation to learn

5. Gaining comfort with interacting with others via the computer[3]

Students who have limited computer experience, or those who are frequently online but have never been a part of an online academic community, are likely to encounter hurdles of one kind or another as they first acclimate to their new surroundings. This book is intended to empower you to overcome these hurdles as you work toward academic success.

❖ ORGANIZATION OF THE BOOK

Some elements of this book are specifically targeted toward those new to online learning, while others may be relevant to both online and traditional learners:

Chapter 1 will address a number of myths that surround online learning.

Chapter 2 walks readers through the process of preparing for online coursework, and navigating the online learning environment.

Chapter 3 provides useful tips to assist students with organizing their time and space to facilitate productivity.

Chapter 4 familiarizes readers with resources that can support them throughout their education.

Chapter 5 describes potential problems and how to solve them.

Chapter 6 helps students identify their personal learning styles and apply that information to personalize their academic experience.

Chapter 7 walks students through the importance of written communications in an online academic environment, and provides tips for successful communication.

Chapter 8 guides students through the process of conducting research.

Chapter 9 explains the importance of properly citing sources, and provides a step-by-step walk-through of doing so.

This book is intended to build readers' confidence as they enter the online classroom. Whether read cover-to-cover or used as a quick-reference when issues are encountered, the information included in this book will support students in making the most of their learning experience. In addition to the best practices that are presented on these pages, students should also walk away with an understanding that:

1. There will be hurdles along the way, and that is okay. These are hurdles, not barriers. They can be overcome.

2. There is no shame in asking for help.

3. It will be worth it.

Welcome to online learning!

❖ NOTES

1. Allen, I. E., & Seaman, J. (2008). Staying the course: Online education in the United States, 2008. Sloan-C: United States. http://www.sloan-c.org/publications/survey/pdf/staying_the_course.pdf

2. Information for Figure 0.1 compiled with data from the following:

Allen, I.E., & Seaman, J. (2008). Staying the course: Online education in the United States, 2008. Sloan-C:United States. http://www.sloan-c.org/publications/survey/pdf/staying_the_course.pdf

Allen, I.E., & Seaman, J. (2007). Online Nation: Five Years of Growth in Online Learning. Sloan-C:United States. http://www.sloan-c.org/publications/survey/pdf/online_nation.pdf

Allen, I.E., & Seaman, J. (2006). Making the Grade: Online Education in the United States, 2006. Sloan-C:United States. http://www.sloan-c.org/publications/survey/pdf/Making_the_Grade.pdf

Allen, I.E., & Seaman, J. (2005). Growing by Degrees: Online Education in the United States, 2005. Sloan-C: United States. http://www.sloan-c.org/publications/survey/pdf/growing_by_degrees.pdf

Allen, I.E., & Seaman, J. (2003). Sizing the Opportunity: The Quality and Extent of Online Education in the United States, 2002 and 2003. Sloan-C:United States.

3. Tyler-Smith, K. (2006). Early attrition among first time elearners: A review of factors that contribute to drop-out, withdrawal and non-completion rates of adult learners undertaking elearning programmes. *MERLOT Journal of Online Learning and Teaching, 2*(2), 73–85.

1

Debunking the Myths
of Online Education

❖ INTRODUCTION

The first task of this text is to ensure that students have a realistic understanding of what it means to be an online learner. It is not unusual for students new to online education to feel uncertain regarding what lies ahead. There may be an initial apprehension about the quality of online education, the relationships that will be developed with instructors and fellow students, or the difficulty of learning the technologies or maintaining the discipline necessary to be successful. At the other extreme are those who walk in with inaccurate beliefs about the ease of online education and as a result do not dedicate enough time to their coursework. Research has shown that students who know what to expect of their online classes are more likely to be successful in their studies.[1] This chapter therefore aims to help you get your bearings as you first begin your online schooling by addressing eight common myths:

- Taking online courses is "settling" for a lesser-quality education.

- I am feeling overwhelmed; online learning must not be for me.

- I don't know my way around a computer: I can't do this!

- With online education, I am "going it alone."

- I am online all the time: This will be easy!

- Online learning requires less time than traditional education.

- Since this is an online course, I can complete the coursework whenever I want.

- My online coursework will not be respected by others.

❖ MYTH #1: TAKING ONLINE COURSES IS "SETTLING" FOR A LESSER-QUALITY EDUCATION

Many students enroll in online classes due to necessity rather than choice. They may live in a rural area and therefore have difficulty accessing a brick-and-mortar campus, or may have to undergo medical treatments that preclude their ability to travel to campus to attend class at a set time each week. Those who are struggling to balance multiple obligations, from single moms to the active military, may find themselves in an online classroom because they feel that it is their only reasonable option for pursuing a degree. Those whose first choice would be to travel to a physical campus may feel an initial disappointment at the need to "settle" for online classes.

Still, the growing consensus is that online learning can rival, or in some cases surpass, the levels of quality and student satisfaction found on brick-and-mortar campuses. The content of the online curriculum is often quite comparable to that found in face-to-face classrooms in terms of assignments and material covered, but the online platform facilitates a broader array of delivery styles and a greater level of interaction among students.

Between the uncompromised quality and the ease and flexibility inherent to being able to access the "classroom" from anywhere with a stable Internet connection, students are increasingly turning to online education by choice rather than necessity. A number of studies have indicated that students feel they receive a higher quality of education or learned more in the online format than in their traditional courses.[2] Some studies comparing students enrolled in the same class in face-to-face relative to online format have found "a greater degree of satisfaction with the delivery of online courses"[3] as a result of these benefits.

❖ MYTH #2: I AM FEELING OVERWHELMED; ONLINE LEARNING MUST NOT BE FOR ME

Many students initially feel a bit apprehensive as they enter their first term of online classes, experiencing some combination of fear and excitement.[4] Those who are returning after an extended period of time away from formal education, or those who plan to juggle their schooling with other responsibilities, may be particularly nervous. They may have concerns about navigating the online classroom, keeping up with the workload, or dedicating the necessary time to their coursework. The good news is that this initial apprehension is entirely normal. It is not unusual to feel uncertainty when adjusting to something new, just as with starting a new job, moving to a new town, or any other new venture.

The apprehension that may surround your first weeks in the online classroom should be embraced as a natural part of taking on a new challenge—simply a stage to work through on the way to achieving academic goals. You have likely used good reasoning in registering for online courses. Perhaps you hoped to improve your computer literacy, find a way to balance your schooling with other obligations, or avoid a costly and lengthy commute. Those who are willing to persevere through these early weeks will reap rewards in the flexibility of the online format and the reduced or eliminated need to travel to a campus.[5]

To ease your transition, take advantage of any orientation materials provided by your school, and take some time to explore the other resources at your disposal, including your school's Web site (see additional guidance in Chapter 2). Understand that it will take some time to adjust to the workload and integrate your schooling with your other responsibilities, but this transition period will pass. Before you know it, you will be feeling at ease in your new environment, and it will have been worth the effort.

> *Learning Tip: As you acclimate to online learning, take things one at a time, and don't be afraid to use the resources available to you.*

❖ MYTH #3: I DON'T KNOW MY WAY AROUND A COMPUTER: I CAN'T DO THIS!

Students who are new to computers may feel particularly nervous about their foray into online education. Becoming a successful online learner involves not only an adjustment to the nature of college coursework but also the ability to navigate the necessary technology, as well as the classroom Web site.[6] Basic skills, such as the ability to conduct searches on the Internet, perform basic computer maintenance, and create, format, and save new documents, will be necessary to stay involved in online courses.

Being new to something is no reason to give up; in fact, it should serve as extra motivation. Basic computer skills are a prerequisite for many positions in the current workforce; by taking some time to learn basic computer skills, you can improve your job marketability before you even complete your first online course. There are plenty of tools available to support those who are new to computers. First, use your contacts—reach out to other students or your main contact at the school to ask whether school-specific materials are available to help you become familiar with the necessary technology. If one of those individuals is willing to walk you through navigation of the online classroom, take them up on the offer, and take lots of notes to facilitate your ability to follow those steps on your own. Also be sure to secure the contact information for technical support.

There are also publicly available resources available to assist those who are new to computers. Local job centers or community colleges may offer computer classes that are free or low-cost. Online tools are also available. If you aren't familiar with how to navigate the Internet, ask someone—perhaps a friend or a librarian at your local library—for assistance in visiting the following sites:

- http://tech.tln.lib.mi.us/tutor—This tutorial covers how to use a mouse for those who are entirely new to computers.

- http://www.gcflearnfree.org—This site provides free online tutorials on computer basics including how to perform computer maintenance, navigate the Windows operating system, and use Internet, e-mail, and common programs such as Microsoft Word, PowerPoint, and Excel.

❖ MYTH #4: WITH ONLINE EDUCATION, I AM "GOING IT ALONE"

As of fall 2007, nearly 4 million students were taking college courses in the United States alone.[7] As an online student, you are part of a growing academic community of those who consider turning on a computer to be an integral part of "attending class." Still, as you sit down in the

Figure 1.1 Goodwill Offers Free Online Computer Classes

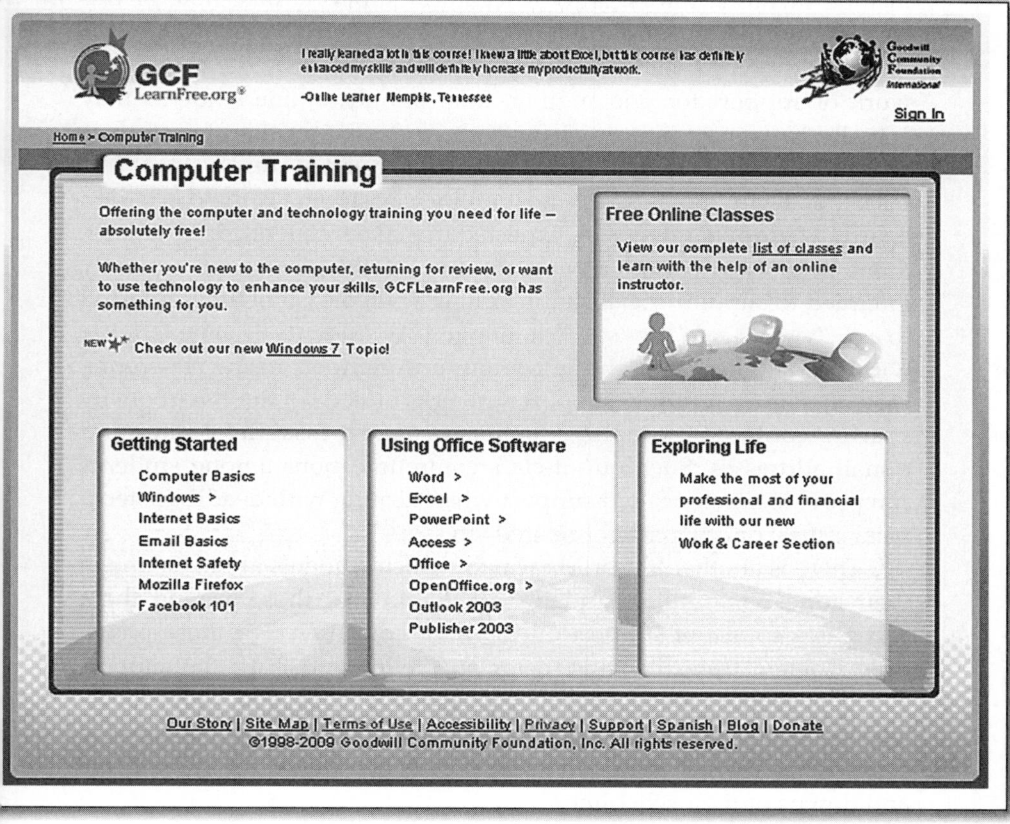

silence of your living room, click into your classroom, and unlike a traditional class see no face aside from, perhaps, your own reflection on the computer screen, it is easy to feel a sense of isolation. If you are surrounded by others who are not in school, you may also feel as though nobody else grasps the extent of the responsibilities on your shoulders, or the stress of meeting academic deadlines.

The truth is that as an online student, you are not alone by any measure. Investing some initial time in clicking around the classroom and other parts of the school Web site will reveal a robust network of resources in place to support you. First and foremost are instructors, whose contact information can typically be located in the classroom or other course-related communications such as e-mails. Instructors are familiar with the learning curve experienced by students new to online learning and are often happy to assist; don't hesitate to reach out to them with questions. Most schools will offer a multitude of other resources as well; while the specifics will vary by institution, they may include mentors, tutors, and/or technical support. Take note of this contact information, and use it to your advantage!

In addition to school resources, students can provide a solid network of support for one another. Interestingly, online students may actually have *more* interaction with their classmates than face-to-face students. Unlike traditional courses, which are often run in lecture format, the "heart and soul" of most online classrooms is the discussion board, where all students are expected to make frequent contributions. Some schools also host a separate area of the classroom explicitly intended to support socialization among students, sometimes referred to as a "virtual cafe" or "student lounge." As students become familiar with one another through the communication tools in the classroom, they often form informal support networks outside of the classroom by sharing contact information such as instant messaging names and e-mail addresses. Such out-of-class communications among students can provide much-needed support when dealing with deadlines, technical issues, or other school-related stressors.[8]

There is another important way in which students are not alone in their education. Online students often find that those around them serve as a source of support during their education. For those physically isolated from their instructor and fellow students, the support garnered from friends and loved ones takes on added significance. Many online students find that their friends and relatives come to play a critical role in providing moral support as they work through the ups and downs of their schooling.

Unfortunately, if you have roommates or live with family members, you may occasionally encounter frustration if the other members of the household fail to respect your need to study. (While this author was attempting to complete her take-home comprehensive exams for her doctoral program, her roommate relaxed in the next room and watched the *Family Guy* at a tempting volume, which did not help her feel supported in her academic endeavors!) It may be necessary to set up "house rules" for certain times each day that are set aside for schoolwork. The television and telephone ringer may need to be off at certain times. It is also a good idea to establish a study space where others know not to interrupt you if the door is closed.

If you encounter an initial sense of isolation as an online student, take some time to appreciate that you can now attend class in your pajamas with your favorite drink or snack close at hand. You can complete your coursework from the comfort of your own home or some other favorite Internet "hot spot" of your choosing (see Chapter 3 for tips on finding suitable workspaces). You can play the radio if it helps you work, without worrying about disrupting the class; similarly, you need not worry about disruptive classmates rendering you unable to hear the instructor. As you enjoy these thoughts, rest assured that these benefits do not truly come at the cost of being alone. Welcome to the large and growing community of online learners!

> *Learning Tip: If you live with others,*
> *set up "house rules" that will support you in your schooling.*

❖ MYTH #5: I AM ONLINE ALL THE TIME: THIS WILL BE EASY!

While some students may be apprehensive because they are new to the online environment, others may feel quite confident based on their level of comfort with technology. The "at-your-fingertips" convenience of online education may contribute to its inaccurate reputation in some circles as an "easy" alternative to traditional coursework, with convenience mistaken by some as an indicator of ease. It is true that an online education is *logistically* easier to access than a physical classroom, particularly for those comfortable with computers; even students who live on campus may be tempted to enroll in an online class or two when the alternative is to trudge to a face-to-face class through the hot sun, torrential rain, or blowing snow.

Still, the myth that being online all the time will make online learning easier has only a small grain of truth to it. If you are online frequently, it likely means that you have a solid Internet connection, which will be helpful as you work through your courses. It may also mean that you have strong computer literacy skills (that you can easily find your way around a Web page), which will also help ease your transition to online education. That being said, technological competence in itself is not enough to carry you through schooling. The difficulty of online classes can vary as widely as it would in a traditional setting. A 12-page paper on the implications of postmodern thought, or a final exam on organizational theory, will not be rendered any easier due to fluency in an online environment. This means that regardless of your comfort level with technology, it is important to budget sufficient time to focus on your schooling—a detail that leads nicely into the next myth.

❖ MYTH #6: ONLINE LEARNING REQUIRES LESS TIME THAN TRADITIONAL EDUCATION

Because of the flexibility of online education, students may take for granted that their online coursework can easily fit into their typical schedule. Some online programs claim that students can earn a degree in their spare time, which perpetuates the myth that students need not allocate any structured time to work on their courses. Students who already know themselves to spend evenings on the computer may envision themselves earning a degree as they simultaneously peruse the Internet and check e-mails, while others with packed schedules may anticipate easily fitting their schooling around other obligations.

There is some truth to the belief that online schooling can save time relative to traditional coursework, but this "time saved" is limited to the elimination of a commute. Online students do not need to concern themselves with traffic jams, slippery roads, or public transit delays, nor account for the significant time that may be required to find a good parking spot near a brick-and-mortar campus. To show up for a face-to-face class at a given time might entail a commute of an hour or longer; to meet with others online may require only five minutes of preparation to make sure that the computer is on and an Internet connection established.

Aside from commuting time, online students have reported that they actually dedicate more time to online courses each week than traditional courses.[9] This may be due to the high expectation for active participation that is common to online courses, or the additional demands of learning course material without the benefit of live meeting times. A quality education entails not only exposure to new information but also taking the time to critically examine that information and ultimately draw meaningful conclusions regarding what has been learned. This process cannot entirely take place while your primary attention is focused on your friends, family, or work, so the successful completion of online courses will require a time commitment.

For those with busy schedules, this is no reason to panic. The good news here—and there is good news!—is that it *is* easier to work online education into one's daily schedule. Online courses do offer a great deal of flexibility, and the time management tips provided in Chapter 3 will support even the busiest of students in taking on their studies full-force. It is simply important to recognize that online courses do require a time commitment, so that students can avoid the trap of "double-booking" themselves.

When tasks seem flexible, it can be easy to fail to allocate specific amounts of time toward those tasks. For example, people who need to send e-mails, conduct research for a class, and take an online quiz may think: "I'll complete those tasks tonight after work," failing to take into account how doing so might conflict with their need to prepare dinner, run errands, and put their children to bed. By the time they sit down to get to work, they may realize that the e-mails take them an hour, the quiz takes a half hour, and the research takes them a full one or two hours (or longer) to complete. Before they know what happened, it is the middle of the night, and they are surprised to still be working on tasks that they expected to complete much earlier in the evening.

As you plan your day, it is important to realize that having more flexibility in *structuring* your time is not the same as actually taking *less* of your time. Regardless of whether you find that you work best in the early hours, late at night, or perhaps during your lunch hour, you will need to find time that you can purely dedicate to your coursework. In the early weeks of your online courses, pay attention to how long it realistically takes to complete various tasks, and plan your schedule accordingly. (See Chapter 3 for time management ideas.)

> *Learning Tip: Allocate sufficient time in your schedule to focus on your schooling.*

❖ MYTH #7: SINCE THIS IS AN ONLINE COURSE, I CAN COMPLETE THE COURSEWORK WHENEVER I WANT

Some students enroll in online courses with the misunderstanding that such courses are always self-paced, and that the material can be completed any time before the end of the semester without penalty. In most cases, this is not true; most online courses will require students to log in a certain number of times each week, and/or to submit materials by specific deadlines spread throughout the term. While this may be an initial disappointment to those who were hoping to have complete control over the structure of their schooling, this format is actually in place for the benefit of the student. Keeping a class moving through the material at a similar pace fosters a sense of community as students focus on the same discussion questions or embark on the same assignments in tandem. This structure also enables instructors to better focus their efforts as they guide students through the complex concepts in each unit.

Distributing deadlines throughout the course also helps to pace those who may otherwise procrastinate until the final days of the term, as well as those who might be tempted to rush through the course at a faster pace than would effectively support an understanding of the material. Particularly in courses that contain cumulative content—where each unit builds on the knowledge gained in the prior unit—this pacing can serve as a safeguard to ensure that students fully understand the concepts from each unit before moving on to more complex material. Because most online courses are not self-paced, it is important to check the classroom carefully for deadlines, and to e-mail the instructor with any questions regarding when work is due. Instructors may be willing to grant extensions for specific assignments if warranted by extenuating circumstances (see Chapter 5 for a full discussion), but in other cases late work may be subject to a penalty, or may not be accepted at all.

Figure 1.2   Sample Calendar for Deadlines

September 2010

SUNDAY	MONDAY	TUESDAY	WEDNESDAY	THURSDAY	FRIDAY	SATURDAY
			1	2	3	3
5	6	7	8	9	10 Unit 8 Discussion Board Postings Due	11
12	13	14	15 Algebra Worksheet Due	16	17 Unit 9 Discussion Board Postings Due	18
19	20	21 Business Comm. Final Due	22	23	24 Unit 10 Discussion Board Postings Due	25
26	27	28	29	30		

❖ MYTH #8: MY ONLINE COURSEWORK WILL NOT BE RESPECTED BY OTHERS

Even as students come to realize the rigor of their own online coursework, they may fear that such courses will receive less respect from prospective employers or graduate schools than those taken in a traditional format. There is a history of stigmatization among online schools; traditional colleges had been slow to explore online education, and traditional educators initially viewed the for-profit institutions that dominated the market with a fair amount of circumspection. With time, though, this stigma has dissipated significantly, with the reputation of schools no longer as closely tied to their instructional modalities.

There are three developments that have contributed significantly to the increased respect given to online courses. First, the line between traditional and online education has blurred substantially. There is no longer a sharp distinction between receiving an "online" versus a "traditional" education. Large online schools such as University of Phoenix and Kaplan University offer courses at a number of brick-and-mortar locations, while traditional schools such as Harvard University and the University of California at Los Angeles are starting to carry online course offerings. Instructors from traditional schools are increasingly serving students online. Even individual classes may not be clearly delineated as "online" versus "traditional," with a number of courses now offered in blended or hybrid formats that entail both online and face-to-face components.

Second, with the sheer growth of online education, more people are gaining an understanding of the rigors of online coursework through personal experience. It is simply becoming more likely that human resource representatives and members of admissions or hiring committees have either personally taken online courses or witnessed friends and loved ones working through the same. Over time, this should continue to chip away at any stigma that might still remain surrounding an online education.

Finally, school administrators are beginning to recognize the power and versatility of the technological tools that support online learning, sometimes beyond what would be possible within a traditional classroom. As will be discussed in Chapter 2, most online courses offer, at a minimum, a discussion area, grade book, and mechanism for electronically submitting assignments; increasingly, though, schools are experimenting with tools that allow more engaging and accessible delivery of course content. Podcasts, live online meetings with audio and/or video components and the use of electronic "white-boards" that resemble the look and function of dry erase boards are gaining respect and acceptance.

❖ CONCLUSION

Online learning appears to be the new wave of education. More people and organizations are starting to recognize the potential for students to receive a solid education online—one that, by some measures, may actually surpass conventional mediums. Students who are entering the online classroom for the first time should be prepared for the challenges that lie ahead but should also find motivation in the knowledge that they are entering a vibrant academic community without having to compromise work-from-home flexibility and convenience.

REFLECTION QUESTIONS

1. What do you see as the benefits of taking online classes?

2. What concerns do you have about your ability to succeed in online classes, and how might you address those concerns?

3. What beliefs do you hold regarding online education, and how do they compare to the information presented in this chapter?

4. Describe an experience that you have had that you initially approached with some apprehension. What did you learn from that experience that you might apply to your schooling?

CHAPTER CHECKLIST

☐ Explore whether your school provides orientation materials; if so, locate and review them.

☐ Reflect on whether you need additional computer training to be successful; if so, locate resources accordingly.

☐ Identify a support system that you can rely upon as you begin your schooling.

☐ If you live with others, establish "house rules" that will facilitate your success.

☐ Examine your schedule, and identify specific times each day that you can dedicate to your studies.

RELATED RESOURCES

Basic Computer Tutorials	www.gcflearnfree.org
Help With Using a Mouse	tech.tln.lib.mi.us/tu

❖ NOTES

1. See review in Stanford-Bowers, D. E. (2008). Persistence in online classes: A study of perceptions among community college stakeholders. *MERLOT Journal of Online Learning and Teaching, 4*(1), 37–50.

2. For example, Dobbs, R. R., Waid, C. A., & del Carmen, A. (2009). Students' perceptions of online courses: The effect of online course experience. *The Quarterly Review of Distance Education, 10*(1), 9–26. See also Hannay, M., & Newvine, T. (2006). Perceptions of distance learning: A comparison of online and traditional learning. *MERLOT Journal of Online Learning and Teaching, 2*(1), 1–11.

3. Page 326 of Roach, V., & Lemasters, L. (2006). Satisfaction with online learning: A comparative descriptive study. *Journal of Interactive Online Learning, 5*(3), 317–332.

4. Conrad, D. L. (2002). Engagement, excitement, anxiety, and fear: Learners' experiences of starting an online course. *The American Journal of Distance Education, 16*(4), 205–226.

5. See, for example, Rodriguez, M. C., Oooms, A., & Montanez, M. (2008). Students' perceptions of online-learning quality given comfort, motivation, satisfaction, and experience. *Journal of Interactive Online Learning, 7*(2), 105–125. See also Tesone, D. V., & Ricci, P. (2008). Student perceptions of Web-based instruction: A comparative analysis. *MERLOT Journal of Online Learning and Teaching, 4*(3), 317–324.

6. Tyler-Smith, K. (2006). Early attrition among first time elearners: A review of factors that contribute to drop-out, withdrawal and non-completion rates of adult learners undertaking elearning programmes. *MERLOT Journal of Online Learning and Teaching, 2*(2), 73–85.

7. Allen, I. E., & Seaman, J. (2008). Staying the course: Online education in the United States, 2008. Sloan-C: United States. http://www.sloan-c.org/publications/survey/pdf/staying_the_course.pdf

8. See, for example, Sparks, P. (2006). Electronic note passing: Enriching online learning with new communications tools. *MERLOT Journal of Online Learning and Teaching, 2*(4), 268–274.

9. Hannay, M., & Newvine, T. (2006). Perceptions of distance learning: A comparison of online and traditional learning. *MERLOT Journal of Online Learning and Teaching, 2*(1), 1–11.

2

Where Do I Start?

❖ INTRODUCTION

Now that you have a better impression of online education more generally, it is time to get started! This chapter walks you through the process of preparing your computer for your online courses and then helps you find your way around the "virtual campus" and online classroom. For those new to computers, this stage may be particularly daunting; by taking things step-by-step, this new endeavor will soon feel manageable. For those who do spend a lot of time online, it is still important to make sure that you have all required programs installed to access your classroom without any issue. Setting aside time to explore your school's Web site also shouldn't be discounted, as some Web sites are less intuitively designed than others; the more you take the time to look around, the less likely you are to miss out on useful resources. This chapter will address the following:

- Technology basics
- Getting comfortable with the online campus
- Exploring the online classroom

❖ TECHNOLOGY BASICS

There are a few basic matters that need to be in order to reduce the likelihood that technology will interfere with your success. You need to secure access to a computer and an Internet connection. You should also install virus protection and any programs specifically required by your school.

Computer Access

It is strongly recommended that you have a reliable computer for your coursework. Some students may be tempted to avoid the cost of purchasing a computer by working at a local library or on a friend's or relative's computer. While these options may be short-term solutions for getting into your classroom (see Chapter 3 for full discussion), they also seriously limit your flexibility and may not afford you adequate time to complete all of your assignments. These options may also preclude you from being able to download and install programs that will be necessary to view all classroom materials.

If you are unsure of whether your computer meets the technological requirements of your school, ask for the assistance of someone who is familiar with computers; in some cases, the school's technical support team may be able to assist. If you plan to invest in a new machine, first check to see whether your school requires any specific type of computer, operating system, and/or software. For example, a program in graphic design may require that students obtain a MacBook Pro, whereas hard-science students may run into compatibility issues if they try to use a Mac.

If you have some flexibility in the type of computer you need and cost is a concern, you may be able to take advantage of the growing number of affordable machines on the market. Desktop computers have come down in price, and a number of companies are now offering miniature computers ("minis") at low cost. "Minis" are similar to laptops in their design but may be pared down in some of their features. Just be sure to investigate whether a computer fits your needs before purchasing one—for example, some of the minis do not have a CD-ROM drive, which may make it more difficult to install required software programs. Explore whether your school's bookstore offers student discounts on computers through its Web site.

Virus Protection

External threats such as viruses and spyware can impact the functioning of your computer. To keep a computer running at its optimal level and to reduce the risk of losing work, take some time now to confirm that you have virus protection; if you do, check the settings to make sure that you are receiving automatic updates. If you have been slow to acquire virus protection for financial reasons, look into the free anti-virus programs available for download; one such product is available at http://free.avg.com.

Internet Connection

Consider availability, speed, and cost when exploring possible Internet services. If you live in a rural area, your options may be limited. Look in your local telephone book for Internet providers, or talk to neighbors to see whether they have recommendations for service in your area. If you live in a larger city, you are more likely to have quite a few options to compare along the criteria of speed and cost.

With a *dial-up connection,* the computer's "modem" dials a number through the standard phone line to establish an Internet connection. Dial-up service tends to be low cost, though it is important to make sure that the number being dialed is local to avoid additional charges if you do not have an unlimited long distance plan.[1] While it may be tempting to pursue this option due to the lower monthly expense, be aware that it will hinder efficiency due to time spent waiting for Internet pages to load and downloads to complete. Dial-up is not recommended unless your area does not have broadband (high-speed) Internet coverage.

A *broadband connection* transmits and receives information at a much higher speed than dial-up. Depending upon your location, a variety of broadband services might be available; broadband connections may be provided through your phone company in the form of "DSL," through your cable company, or, most common in rural areas, via satellite.[2] If at all possible, try to secure broadband service. Investing in a broadband connection may be the single best investment that you can make in the efficiency of your online coursework. If the cost seems prohibitive, call Internet providers to see whether they can offer a discounted rate for new customers, or explore whether investing in a "bundle" package (which provides a single bill for multiple services, such as phone, Internet, and cable television) would be financially beneficial for your household.

> *Learning Tip: If at all possible, subscribe to a broadband Internet service for your home.*

Another option for Internet service is to invest in a *mobile broadband plan* through a cellular service provider. Much like cell phone service, these services require an initial investment in equipment (an adapter), as well as a monthly service plan. The adapter enables users to connect from anywhere within certain service areas, but there is a risk of encountering "dead zones" (areas that do not receive a signal) or dropped connections similar to those experienced by cell phone users. Mobile broadband is ideal for those who use a laptop and travel frequently within their provider's coverage area, since it precludes the need to search for an Internet connection while traveling. Because these connections may not be reliable from inside buildings or in rural areas, though, most subscribers to mobile broadband will have this service in addition to their home Internet service.

Specialized Programs

Once you are set up with a reliable computer and an Internet connection, there may be specific programs or software that you need to install. Schools make use of a wide variety of technological tools to deliver course content, allowing instructors to post anything from supplementary documents to audio or visual presentations. As you click around the campus and, ultimately, the classroom itself, you will likely find reference to tools that you will need to install in order to view the necessary materials for your online class. Many common requirements can be downloaded for free:

- Adobe Reader—www.adobe.com

- Flash player—www.adobe.com

- Java—www.java.com

- QuickTime—www.apple.com/quicktime/download

- RealPlayer—www.real.com

- Windows Media Player—www.microsoft.com/windows/windowsmedia/player

Some schools will offer a "system check" for compatibility, which, if clicked, will provide you with an at-a-glance report of any programs that you may be lacking.

Finally, take note of whether you are expected to purchase any software, such as Microsoft Office, for your courses. Software compatibility is an important requisite for online success; a student may not earn credit for even the highest quality work if the instructor is unable to open the assignment because of system incompatibility. If you are unable to afford a required software package, check to see whether your school's bookstore offers a discount. Your advisor may also have tips for handling this situation.

❖ GETTING COMFORTABLE WITH THE ONLINE CAMPUS

Once your computer is set up and your Internet connection established, it's time to start exploring! Just as a student might take time to wander a physical campus to learn the location of the library, classroom buildings, and coolest hangouts, the first task of any online student should be to take a tour of the new "virtual" surroundings. This is a process of exploration; even if you are new to online learning but not to your particular school, spend some time "digging down" through different areas of your school's Web site to learn which resources can be accessed remotely. You may be surprised to find resources that you didn't know existed, or that you had not realized were accessible online.

Depending upon the institution, there may be a great deal to explore outside of the classroom. Most schools will provide some library access online, and others may offer online bookstores, directories, tutoring services, or social areas. As you click around the Web site, make a list of the important resources that you find, and record how you accessed them. For links on the school's public Web site, utilize the "bookmarks" or "favorites" feature on your Web browser to save links for important resources, as this will save time when you need to access them in the future. (This feature may not work properly for pages accessed after logging into a password-protected area of the Web site.)

As you peruse your school's Web site, write down any phone numbers that you find for technical support, financial aid, the registrar's office, and other important offices. Post these numbers in a prominent place and program them into your cell phone if you have one. If you have difficulty finding a phone number for technical support, look closely at the login page through which the online courses are accessed; the contact information for technical support is often posted there, sometimes through a "help," "support center," or "contact us" link.

Learning Tip: Maintain a notebook or folder for important information relevant to your schooling.

As you learn your way around, it may be helpful to know that predominantly online schools are likely to offer a single "portal"—one login page—through which students can access a multitude of services, such as the school library, registration, and their classrooms. If you are taking online courses through a traditional institution, resources may be more diffuse on the site. You may need different login information to access library, registration, e-mail, and the online classroom, and may need to click through links labeled "Learning," "Students," "Current Students," "Academics," or some similar title to find these resources. In some cases, the login page for online classes will be found through a link for the school's distance education or returning student program.

The more comfortable you are with the layout of your school's Web site, the easier it will be to access resources when you need them. After taking some time to explore, you should be feeling less "lost." Those still feeling uncertain of where to click for which services may simply need more time to become adequately familiar with the site. There is no shame in taking a while to become fully comfortable with finding your way around; take your time, and enjoy learning about the many resources at your disposal!

❖ EXPLORING THE ONLINE CLASSROOM

Once you feel secure in the technical requirements expected and the general "virtual" environment provided by your school, the next step is to explore the actual classroom. As one author stated, "Many students do not realize that beginning [class] consists simply of clicking—in solitude—on a course Web site."[3] This is an exciting step, as the online classroom will contain information about the material that will be covered throughout the term, as well as what will be expected of students to complete the class successfully.

The classroom will be laid out somewhat differently depending upon whether your school utilizes Blackboard, eCollege, Desire2Learn (D2L), Moodle, or some other platform to host its courses. These are all simply references to companies or organizations that provide the technological framework on which the school has built its online courses. These companies can be thought of as the technological architects of the online classroom—they establish the types of features available, such as quizzes, announcements, discussion boards, and, to a great extent, the classroom layout and aesthetics. It can be useful to know which school your platform uses, both to understand references made by the instructor (i.e., "log into the Blackboard site") and to enable you to perform Internet searches for additional assistance if you encounter difficulty navigating the course layout.

Since some courses will be more intuitively structured than others, just as with learning the online "campus" environment, take some time to simply click around the classroom. If you are new to computers, don't be afraid of doing harm by these explorations—if you ever "get lost" on the classroom site, look for a "cancel" option, or utilize the "back" arrow on your Internet browser to get to the previous screen. If that doesn't work, use the red "X" in the upper right-hand corner of the

Figure 2.1	Screen Shot of Online Classroom

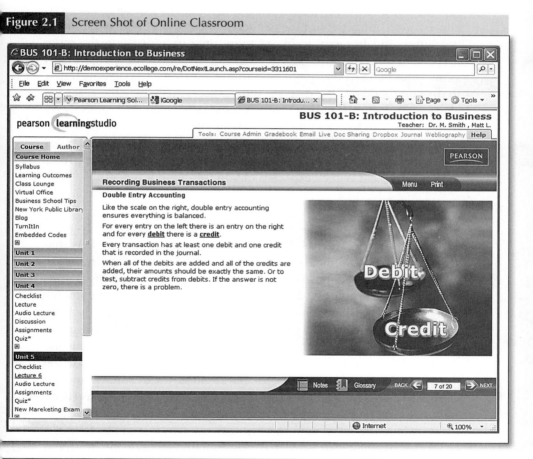

Source: Screen shot of Pearson LearningStudio—Campus Edition.

Internet browser to close that browser window, and then simply open a new window to log back into the classroom.

❖ KNOWING WHAT TO LOOK FOR

Once you have had the chance to explore your classroom, it's time to get organized for a successful term. A good starting point is to focus on answering these questions:

- What is due when?
- How do I submit it?

Knowing these details at the start of the term will lessen anxiety, allow you to budget your time in a manner consistent with assignment deadlines, and free you to invest more time in addressing the more involved question of what it will take to do well on those assignments. While your main focus should be learning—research has demonstrated that online students tend to be more successful when their goal is learning, not simply getting through the class[4]—even the highest-level learner will run into significant problems if he or she fails to realize when work is due, or how to submit it! The journey of a thousand miles truly does begin with a single step, which in this case is simply to understand what will be expected of you throughout the term.

Where to Look

In your trek to answer the first two questions at hand—what is due when, and how it needs to be submitted—examine the following areas.

Syllabus. The syllabus is a document that typically contains an outline of the course, a list or detailed description of relevant assignments and readings, instructor contact information, and relevant course policies. Take the time to read the syllabus carefully, and if possible, print a hard copy for future reference. This document is often viewed as the "contract" between instructors and students, and it is likely to be the most centralized source of useful information on deadlines and/or expectations. If you can't find the course syllabus, it is time to either roll up your sleeves to engage in a more aggressive search of the classroom or to reach out to your instructor to ask where it can be found.

Announcements. Instructors may post announcements in the classroom with expectations for the course, to either clarify or expand upon what had been included on the syllabus. In some platforms, announcements will be readily visible as soon as students click into the classroom; in others, there may be an "announcements" link that needs to be selected in order to view the instructor's communications. Not all classrooms will have this feature, but if you are unsure of whether it exists, it may be worthwhile to double-check with the instructor or fellow students to make sure that you don't miss any key communications.

E-mails from the instructor. Without the ability to rely on frequent face-to-face meetings with students, some instructors make use of e-mail to explain concepts or clarify expectations or deadlines. In many cases, these e-mails will go to each student's school e-mail address (if the school has provided one), making it important to know whether your school has provided you with an e-mail account, and if so how to log in to check messages. If you need assistance with this, reach out to technical support or one of your other school contacts. There have been cases where students have missed important instructor communications because they were unaware that they had a school-provided e-mail account, or because they failed to check that account frequently. For those who simply prefer to use preexisting personal e-mail accounts, explore whether there is a way to set up message forwarding so that messages sent to your school address appear in your preferred account.

> *Learning Tip: Find out whether you have a school-provided e-mail account; if so, check it frequently.*

Some learning platforms will enable students to enter a preferred e-mail address to which any instructor e-mails would be sent. If you see a "user information," "my account," or "profile" option when you log into your classroom Web site, select this option to see whether you have control over the e-mail address on file. If so, be sure to enter an e-mail address that you check frequently.

Other possible resources. During your classroom explorations, take note of other resources that may ultimately support your success in the classroom, such as helpful links, documents, or announcements. Some instructors may provide weekly "checklists" of what needs to be completed, post sample papers to more clearly display what they expect of student work, or refer students to Web sites that will aid them in learning the material. After thoroughly exploring the classroom, if there is still a sense of uncertainty regarding what is due when, it may be time to contact the instructor with the contact information that was found on the syllabus or elsewhere in the classroom.

What to Look For: Common Gradable Components

As with face-to-face classes, online courses can vary substantially in their assignment structures and expectations, which is why it is important to explore all corners of the classroom to feel confident in what needs to be submitted by which dates. Many types of gradable work will mirror what might be assigned in a traditional classroom; in fact, some instructors teach the same courses both online and in person and may assign nearly identical work in both formats. Online courses may entail exams or quizzes and are likely to require the submission of papers, presentations, or other types of assignments.

The largest divergence in the gradable elements of online courses relative to face-to-face is likely to be in the expectations for student participation. Without the ability to monitor attendance by simply glancing around a physical classroom, online instructors have identified a number of other ways to measure and grade student involvement. It is therefore important to not simply look for the deadlines of major projects, but to also understand the expectations put forth for logging into the classroom and participating in discussions. In the broadest sense, required participation in an online course may include *synchronous* expectations, *asynchronous* expectations, or both.

For courses that entail a *synchronous* component, students are expected to meet with their instructor and classmates at set dates and times to engage in "real time" interaction with one other. For courses that are entirely online, these meetings are facilitated by technology. The class may be asked to click into a common area online at the same time, or to dial a teleconference number. Meetings that take place on the Internet might entail typing, audio, video, or some combination. If your courses contain a synchronous component facilitated by technology, be sure to familiarize yourself with any technological requirements before the first class period.

If the class materials make reference to a given meeting time—for example, "Mondays at 9 pm ET"—take note of the meeting time and find out how to access the relevant meeting area. Also, if your school has students from across the country, be sure to account for time zone differences in planning your attendance. Finally, keep in mind that for courses with synchronous meetings, attendance alone may not be enough for a good grade; in most cases, there will also be an expectation that students actively engage in the interactions.

For students taking hybrid or blended courses—those that have both online and face-to-face components—pay special attention to the expectations for attendance. In some cases, attendance at the on-ground meetings may be optional, but in others it may be factored into the course grade. For those who may be balancing school with other responsibilities, it is important to plan ahead for these meetings. Block off the dates and times on your calendar, and make any arrangements for child care or transportation that may be necessary to be in attendance.

Learning Tip: If your class has a synchronous component, make sure that you know how to attend. Don't forget to account for your time zone in planning your attendance.

In *asynchronous* communications, students are expected to participate in discussions or message board exchanges with other students that are not in "real time." Typically the instructor will post a question to which students can respond within a given, broad time frame. The entire class need not be present at the exact same time. For example, students may have one week to participate in a given discussion; some may post early in the day and others late in the evening, and some on Monday and others on Tuesday or Wednesday. Even though students are not necessarily logged into the classroom and participating at the same time as one another, they still engage with each other. As students log in, they can view the contributions of those who have participated before them and post their own responses to the main question and to their classmates. If your class has a requirement for participation in asynchronous discussions, make the most of it, as this is truly the best of both worlds! This area presents the ability to engage in meaningful and interesting exchanges with your classmates, while also allowing the flexibility of working (within broad confines) on your own schedule.

For classes that require participation in a discussion board, the syllabus or other classroom materials should include guidance regarding expectations for the length and frequency of your contributions. Instructors may require a certain length or number of postings and may also have specific expectations for the distribution of students' participation throughout the week. For example, you may be expected to make three contributions of approximately 200 words each, and to make those contributions on at least two separate days of the week. Pay attention to the stated expectations, as they may vary from one class to another. Also keep in mind that discussion board contributions should be thoughtful, constructive, and respectful in nature (see additional guidance in Chapter 7), and specific instructors may require that students support their contributions with research.

Deadlines in online classes. As explained in Chapter 1, most online courses are not self-paced. In fact, online courses are likely to have a higher expectation for student involvement than face-to-face classes, resulting in more frequent deadlines for assignments, exams, quizzes, and/or discussion board postings. In order to provide students with an incentive to keep pace with the class, instructors may apply a late penalty to work submitted after the deadline, or may refuse to accept late work altogether. (Chapter 3 offers tips for organizing your time to meet deadlines. See Chapter 5 for how to address legitimate issues that may interfere with your ability to meet deadlines.) In order to submit work on time, you should become comfortable with exactly when the work must be submitted, as well as the process for doing so.

Unlike traditional courses in which students simply submit work "in class" on a given day, most online course deadlines will specify both a time and date by which work needs to be completed. Because online courses sometimes enroll students from diverse geographic areas, students should be alert to any reference to a particular time zone in the stated deadline. For example, a school may require that the assignments for each week be submitted by "Sunday evening at 10:59 pm ET." Here, the "ET" designates "Eastern Time"—students in the eastern time zone would need to submit their work by 10:59 pm, but those in other time zones would need to account for the time difference in order to avoid receiving a late penalty. Those in the central time zone would need to submit by 9:59 pm local time, those in the mountain time zone would need to turn in their work by 8:59 pm, and so forth. If you have any question regarding how to account for your time zone to ensure that your work is submitted on time, don't hesitate to reach out to your instructor for assistance.

Finally, in order to meet deadlines, take some time to make sure that you know *how* your work needs to be submitted. Papers or essay exams are usually submitted through a feature in the classroom called something to the effect of "digital drop box" or "assignment manager," whereas discussion board contributions will be assessed based on what you have posted to the discussion board. In rare instances, you may be asked to submit work in hard copy, either on campus (for hybrid or blended courses) or by mail. Read the course materials carefully and complete your first few weeks of assignments slightly ahead of the deadline to ensure that you are comfortable with the submission process. This gives you some leeway if you run into technical issues or have any questions regarding how to submit. Notify your instructor immediately if you run into any issues or questions.

> *Learning Tip: Contact your instructor immediately if you encounter any questions regarding what is expected or how to submit your work.*

Figure 2.2 Time Zone Map

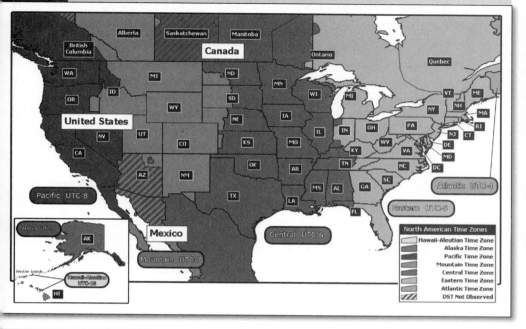

Source: Image from nist.time.gov.

❖ CONCLUSION

After taking the steps outlined in this chapter, you should be feeling much more comfortable with whether your computer setup is consistent with the requirements of your school. You should now have spent time navigating your school's Web site and finding your way around the online classroom. You should also be familiar with the types of work that will be expected of you throughout the term, when that work is due, and how to submit it. If you feel any uncertainty regarding these aspects of your class, now is the time to contact your instructor with questions. Remember, you are not in this alone!

REFLECTION QUESTIONS

1. What questions did you encounter as you explored the online classroom, and how can you get those questions answered?

2. What types of resources did you find on your school's Web site?

3. Do you feel comfortable with what is due when, and how to submit? If not, what do you need to do to get that information?

CHAPTER CHECKLIST

☐ Confirm that your computer has (1) a reliable Internet connection, (2) virus protection, and (3) any programs required by your school.

☐ Establish a notebook or folder with the contact information and directions for accessing school-related resources such as the library, your e-mail account, and technical support.

☐ Print and read a copy of your syllabus.

☐ Identify deadlines for the course, and take notes on how work needs to be submitted.

☐ If your course contains reference to time zones, calculate when you will need to submit your work or (if applicable) appear for class.

RELATED RESOURCES

Adobe Acrobat, Flash Player	www.adobe.com
Free Virus Protection	http://free.avg.com
Java	www.java.com
QuickTime	www.apple.com/quicktime/download
RealPlayer	www.real.com
Time Zone Converter	http://www.worldtimezone.com/time-usa12.php
Windows Media Player	www.microsoft.com/windows/windowsmedia/player

❖ NOTES

1. Levine, J. R., Levine-Young, M., & Baroudi, C. (2007). *The Internet for Dummies* (11th ed.). Hoboken, NJ: Wiley Publishing.

2. Levine, J. R., Levine-Young, M., & Baroudi, C. (2007). *The Internet for Dummies* (11th ed.). Hoboken, NJ: Wiley Publishing.

3. See page 206 of Conrad, D. L. (2002). Engagement, excitement, anxiety, and fear: Learners' experiences of starting an online course. *The American Journal of Distance Education, 16*(4), 205–226.

4. See page 8 of Davies, R. S. (2003). Learner intent and online courses. *The Journal of Interactive Online Learning, 2*(1), 1–10.

3

Getting Organized

❖ INTRODUCTION

Online courses offer students flexibility and convenience. Even as students work to meet deadlines, they also largely get to determine where and when to complete their coursework. There is great freedom inherent to this format, but the reduction or elimination of face-to-face meetings can make it "far too easy for [students] to put off studying for their online courses."[1] This places the responsibility on students to figure out where and when they work best, and to allocate sufficient time to their studies. Since completing work for online courses can actually take more time each week than traditional courses, and online students are likely to be juggling a number of other obligations, this task may initially seem quite daunting. Fortunately, a number of steps can be taken to most efficiently balance coursework with other life responsibilities. This chapter provides ideas for how to organize school materials, locate suitable workspaces, and find ways to mold your coursework around other obligations. By the end of this chapter, you should have a good feel for how to most effectively complete your studies.

❖ GETTING ORGANIZED

Settling into a nice coffee shop with an interesting textbook may sound like a good way to study, but the scenario may lose some appeal if preceded by a half-hour frantic search for that textbook, and another few minutes of hunting around for a notepad and working pen, only to get to the coffee shop and realize that you have forgotten to pack much-needed highlighters. Organization can be difficult for online students as they often study "on the go." Many online students also split their time and attention among many responsibilities, which may add to the challenge of staying organized. Without a sustainable strategy, countless hours may be spent simply finding what is needed to study. Your time is valuable; as such, this section sets forth some easy-to-follow ideas for preventing wasted hours.

Organization in the Home

As you prepare for your classes, you are likely to obtain a number of school-related materials—anything from computers to staples, binders to flash drives. While students have widely diverse living conditions and study habits, the one universal principle for staying organized is simply this: Keep all of your school-related materials in one location. For most students, this will be a dedicated office area centered on their home computer. Still, even those who study "on the go" should establish a "home base" for school-related items. While not ideal, if space is at a premium, this location may be as simple as a dedicated crate that can be slid under a table, or a wall-mounted shelf.

If you always know where to go when you need something for school, it will save time that might otherwise be lost digging through drawers or running from room to room in search of an item. Even those who don't have the time to file materials neatly every day will benefit from taking a moment to return materials to home base when they are done using them. Done consistently, this will limit setup time and maximize actual study time.

Take some time to brainstorm about the items that would be useful to have on-hand to support your studies, such as the following:

- Textbooks, school notes, and other academic materials
- A flash drive, backup hard drive, or some other device to back up electronic files
- A calendar to help you keep track of due dates and other responsibilities

- Basic office supplies, such as working pens, highlighters, paper, and a stapler

- Binders, folders, or other organizational tools for your notes and printed materials

- Index cards or other study aids

While simply keeping materials in a centralized location will go a long way in saving time, more refined organizational strategies are encouraged, especially if you are managing a heavy course load. Some students may work best with hanging files in a file cabinet; others may prefer to maintain a folder or binder for each class. Select the organizational style that appeals to you the most, and stick to it.

> *Learning Tip: Keep all of your school-related materials in one place.*

On-the-Road Study Pack

Even with a properly maintained "home base," those who prefer to work away from home may find themselves occasionally reaching their study destination only to discover that they have forgotten some key item. If you travel frequently or simply prefer not to work at home, keep a bag pre-packed with some basic office supplies, such as pens, paper, a USB drive, and any other tools that may aid your efficiency. Also pack items for your comfort, such as facial tissue or a few dollars for incidentals while you are studying. If there are items that will be unpacked between study trips, such as a laptop and charger, keep a checklist in the bag that you can run through before you leave home to make sure that nothing is forgotten. If you find yourself at your destination wishing that you had brought an item that was not on your list, add it right away so that you can be better prepared next time.

Electronic Organization

Organizing electronic files on your computer is as important as, if not more so than, organizing hard-copy study materials. Store your school-related electronic files in a centralized area so that you know where to find them when needed. Make sure that your file names are appropriately descriptive of their content. It is not unusual for students to first apply file names such as "paper" to their schoolwork; as they accumulate more files, they end up investing time in trying to figure out whether "paper1" or "paper" is the file that they need, or which file is the latest draft of their work. One possible naming convention is to include the name of your course and the specific assignment in each file name, such as "Chemistry101 Midterm." If you like to save multiple versions of your work as you make revisions, integrate the date of the draft as well: "Chemistry101 Midterm 10 23 09." Dating your drafts helps you avoid losing track of whether your most recent file was "new draft," "new new draft," or "draft 2!"

Figure 3.1   An Organized Computer Folder

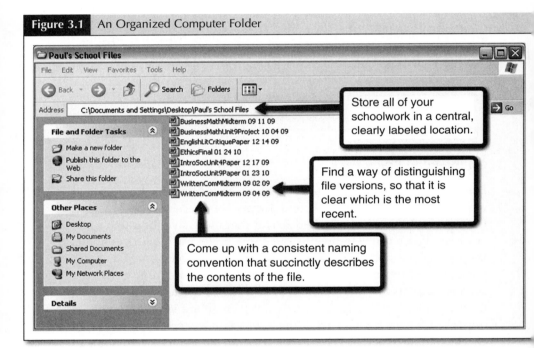

❖ WHERE TO FIND THE SPACE

Once you have some idea as to how your study materials will be organized, there still remains the task of figuring out where to study. Some people work quite well at home, sitting on the couch or settling into a home office. Others may find it difficult to concentrate at home and prefer to go elsewhere to study. This section walks through a four-step process to identify work spaces that match your needs and preferences:

1. Brainstorm
2. Assess

3. Experiment

4. Reflect and Adjust

Step 1: Brainstorm

When first working to identify suitable study locations, compile a comprehensive list of possibilities. Make a list of various rooms in your home and different areas in the community that can be easily accessed. Even students who like the structure of studying in the same place may sometimes need to turn to a "plan B" if there is a temporary Internet outage or a conflict over space with roommates or family members. Others may want to alternate work locations frequently to stay motivated, as they may feel stymied if they need to sit at the same desk day after day. Some students may prefer to vary locations by the type of task that needs to be completed; for example, they may read well at a library but prefer to complete other school assignments at home.

Since the goal at this stage is to come up with as many work areas as possible, think about the buildings that you may pass each day, such as libraries, restaurants, or coffee shops. Just about any place with a seating area is a potential location for studying. This author once had difficulty finding Internet access while spending the summer in a small town, only to find that a local gas station with restaurant-style booths also offered free wireless Internet for customers. Since the gas station was open 24/7, it turned out to be an ideal study situation. Don't rule out any possibilities at this stage.

The only cautionary note: While it may be tempting to check into your online classroom if you have a computer at work, please discuss this with your supervisor before doing so. Find out whether it is acceptable to study during down time, or during your breaks or after hours. If your employer is agreeable, you may find your workplace to be a good place to get coursework done, and it should be included on your list of possible study locations. If not, please find other ways of managing your studies. Many employers have strict policies regarding the use of their technology, and they may be able to monitor which sites you visit from your computer. As tempting as it may be to bend the rules, it isn't likely to be worth the risk of the loss of your employment.

> *Learning Tip: Secure your employer's approval before using work resources for your schooling.*

Step 2: Assess

Once you have identified a wide array of possible study locations, it is time to more critically evaluate which of your options will be most conducive to productivity. You may have a nice dining room table with good lighting that would seem to be perfect for studying, but if it is located in a high-traffic area of your household, it may be difficult to concentrate. Consider the following dimensions:

- Comfort—Consider lighting, temperature, noise level, and comfortable seating.

- Accessibility—Can you be there during the hours that you work best?

- Affordability—Is there any cost associated with the location?

- Technology—Is this a location that will enable work on the computer?

If a particular location is appealing to you but you have concerns about some aspect of the environment, consider whether that aspect is within your control. If you find libraries too quiet, an MP3 player may provide a simple solution. If you are distracted by poor temperature control in a particular room of your home, you may not be able to buy new windows or invest in new insulation, but you could arrange to keep a sweater or sweatshirt nearby if things are too cold, or buy an inexpensive fan and keep a beverage cooler on-hand if the room is too warm. Minor adjustments can go a long way!

Step 3: Experiment

Once you have settled on a handful of desirable work areas, consider spending some time trying to work in each of the most viable locations. If you prefer to work from a stable location, then you may quickly settle on a home workspace; still, it may be worth trying another location or two so that you have some comparison of where you are best able to concentrate. For those who feel stifled by the idea of sitting at a desk for hours, engage in a bit of trial-and-error to find out what does foster your productivity. Focus on what feels right to you, rather than forcing yourself to work where you feel you "should" in order to be successful. Some prefer a desk, whereas others work better when they are able to sit on the floor and spread their work around, or settle into a comfortable chair with their book or laptop.

Step 4: Reflect and Adjust

As you try each work area, take some time to reflect on how well you are able to concentrate in each location, and pay attention to the aspects of each environment that have been distracting. Keep in mind that sometimes preferred work conditions will not actually be the most conducive to productivity; for example, some may want to take advantage of the freedom of online learning by working with the radio or television on in the background, even though they consistently get little done while doing so. Remember, the more you can focus on your work, the less time that it will take to complete, so be quick to make adjustments where you notice that you aren't working at your optimum.

> *Learning Tip: Reflect realistically on how productive you are in different work spaces, and adjust your habits accordingly.*

❖ SPECIAL CONSIDERATIONS WHEN WORKING AT HOME

Many students will end up doing much of their studying at home, as the home is, theoretically, easy to access and available 24/7. Still, there may be some limitations to when and exactly where you are able to "set up office." The factors that you should consider include the following:

- Internet connection
- Available space
- Comfort
- Household patterns of use

Internet Connection

When determining where to set up a workspace, keep in mind the limitations set by your Internet connection. While you will spend some time studying materials or working on assignments that may not necessitate being online, much of your work is likely to take place on the Internet. Depending upon whether you have a dial-up, DSL, or cable connection, you may be limited to setting up your computer near a phone outlet or cable hook-up. If the location of your phone or cable connection is a high-traffic area of your home or otherwise unsuitable for productivity, you might consider investing in a wireless network so that you have more freedom regarding where you can do your computer work.

A wireless network allows individuals to access the Internet from within a certain range of a wireless router without having to plug the computer directly into the phone line or cable line. Three things are needed to have a wireless network in the home: Internet service, a wireless router, and a computer with "wi-fi" (wireless) capability. The Internet connection (phone or cable line) plugs into the wireless router instead of directly into the computer. The router acts much like the base unit of a cordless phone; it converts information that comes through the lines into a wireless radio signal that can be read by wi-fi compatible computers that are within a certain range of the device.

Most laptops now come with wi-fi capabilities built in. Setting up a wi-fi connection at home for use with a laptop can provide you with more freedom to work from where you feel most comfortable. A wireless connection can be useful for a desktop computer, as it gives you more freedom regarding where to situate your workspace. Having a wireless-enabled laptop also allows you to take advantage of any "wi-fi hot spots" around your community. (See the section on working away from home for more information on "hot spots.") If you are using an older laptop or desktop, adapters are available to enable wireless capabilities.

Available Space

The location that you choose as your primary work area in the home should have enough space for basic office supplies and some way of keeping textbooks, files, and binders on-hand and organized. If you do have a wireless network, identify a location in your home that will allow sufficient space for these materials while also being away from high-traffic areas to minimize distractions when you are trying to concentrate.

Comfort

Consider the level of motivation that you will have in going to a particular room to study. The author of this book once designated the smallest room in the house as a "home office," only to be continually drawn to a different room that had greater aesthetic appeal (and a fireplace). Try to situate yourself in a location that you will enjoy, or, if your household situation necessitates otherwise, take steps to increase the appeal of the area where you will be working.

Household Patterns of Use

In assessing the suitability of your workspace, be realistic regarding when other members of the household may need to use that space, and whether those needs are in conflict with your study schedule. Conflicts over the use of the room or a shared home computer can be avoided by setting up a household schedule. Consider allocating the use of space for different purposes at different times, or arrange your schedule so that you are working while others are sleeping or away from home. If you find yourself having difficulty concentrating on your studies when others are home, don't give up—get creative! Many online students have reported using the bathroom to study; they may choose to complete their assigned readings while taking a bath or simply sit on the floor with a textbook or their laptop and enjoy the refuge that they find behind a locked door.

❖ FINDING AN OFFICE IN THE COMMUNITY

Some students prefer to exploit the flexibility of online courses by "taking it on the road." The criteria for assessing public study locations are similar to those that might be used in finding a workspace in the home, though the context is a bit different.

Is the work area easily accessible? Consider first whether a given location will be available during the hours that you would prefer to study. Some students sign up for online courses with the assumption that they can complete coursework at the local library, only to discover that the library is closed during the hours that they need to study. Others are quite pleased to discover local restaurants that are open into the late hours of the night and welcoming of students who settle into a booth for a few hours with a book or laptop so long as they order a cup of coffee or some other menu item.

Does the work area offer Internet access? Since online coursework inherently necessitates an Internet connection to complete at least some tasks, if you own a wi-fi enabled laptop take some time to inquire with local libraries, coffee shops, and bookstores to see whether they offer wireless Internet. This knowledge will be useful even if you have Internet service at home; many have been grateful for the connections available at local libraries or coffee shops when they experience an Internet outage or simply need a change of environment to maintain their motivation. Since not all businesses will advertise their wireless connection, it may be worthwhile to call them directly—this author relied on the wireless Internet connection set up for customers at a local restaurant for a good part of a year, which she only learned of from speaking to a waitress. As you investigate potential "wi-fi hot spots," be aware that not all of them will provide free connections. Some will charge users a fee by the minute, hour, or day. When users first attempt to access the Internet in these locations, they encounter a screen that requires the entry of credit card information before they can proceed to access other Internet sites.

While computer and Internet access are important in looking at the "big picture" in online courses, a potential work area should not be ruled out solely because of a lack of Internet access. For those who have hard-copy textbooks or print their e-books or other online materials, reading can be done from anywhere; in fact, many people spend so much time online that they may prefer to complete readings in an area that does not have a computer. This is where areas such as a yard, porch, or deck might come in handy, particularly for those who live in areas with nice climates or those who have "cabin fever" after spending cold months indoors. For students who are fortunate enough to be able to afford a laptop and a wireless broadband card (discussed in Chapter 2), even online work might be taken to the great outdoors.

Is the work area comfortable enough to facilitate your productivity? Pay attention to the feel of the work environments that you try. Students may believe that they have found a good work environment, failing to realize how significantly they are distracted by seemingly minor details. Motivation to work may be influenced by "environmental elements such as quiet, heat, and/or light."[2] A location that has too much background noise, or one that is too silent, may interfere with productivity. It is easy to be distracted by temperatures that are too warm or too cold. This is where the self-reflection comes in; it is important to identify barriers to productivity so that they might be addressed, either through minor adjustments to work habits—bringing headphones to a work location that is otherwise too silent or earplugs for a work location that is too loud, for example—or by switching to a new work environment entirely.

❖ WHERE TO FIND THE TIME

Working efficiently involves more than just organizing work materials; it is about organizing your time as well. There are a few tricks to using your time most effectively and other ways of literally "finding" time that might otherwise be wasted throughout the day.

Scheduling Your Studies

Take some time to map out your typical daily schedule. Be realistic about the time that you usually spend working, with friends or family, sleeping, or taking care of household chores. Consider which of these time spans can be adjusted to accommodate schoolwork. You may need to speak with others in your life, such as your employer, spouse, or even your children, to ask them for support as you schedule your studies. Try to identify a number of potential blocks of time long enough to enable you to immerse yourself into your schoolwork.

While it is easy to assume that you can simply stay up later or wake up earlier to complete your assignments, consider the impact of getting less sleep. Everyone has very real biological limitations to what they can do. If you find yourself losing so much sleep that you have difficulty thinking clearly, take some time to reexamine your schedule to identify other components that might be eliminated or rendered less time-consuming. If you find that you work best early in the morning or late at night while others sleep, then take advantage of your natural schedule but commit to taking a nap sometime during the day. It is common for people to think that they "don't have time for naps," but any work that is done while tired is bound to take longer than work completed while fully alert. Naps can actually result in individuals having more time in the day since each task will take less time to complete.

While it is important to dedicate solid blocks of time to studying and completing assignments throughout the week, there are also periods of "lost time" that you may find throughout the day that can be exploited.

The waiting game. You call your insurance company, telephone service provider, or technical support for assistance, and then you wait. And wait. And wait. Your frustration grows as you watch the minutes pass on the clock, and your mind flashes with all of the other things that you could be doing with that time. Or perhaps you go to a doctor's appointment, and you find that things are running behind. And so you wait. You put laundry into the washing machine, and you wait for it to be done. You place dinner in the oven, and you wait.

In these situations, there are indeed better things that you could be doing! These are great opportunities to sneak in some reading or research for class. When you go to the doctor's office, pack some books or articles that need to be read. If you are about to make a phone call that may likely result in the "waiting game," grab some reading for school first, or, if all of your work is online, make the phone call near your computer so that you can make some discussion board postings.

If your phone has the capability, place it on "speaker" so that you can listen for when your call is taken without having to actually hold the phone. If you are going to the laundromat or plan to spend some time in the kitchen, take your textbook or laptop with you. It isn't recommended that you get into any big projects when playing the "waiting game" since your concentration is likely to be interrupted, but if you can make a few discussion board postings or do a few pages of reading, it is that much less that you will need to do later.

The work break. If you work more than a few hours a day at a job, you likely receive periodic breaks. If you use this time wisely, you will have less to complete once you get home at the end of the day. Pack a book or some articles that you need to read, just as you might for the doctor's waiting room. If you have a job that entails a lot of down-time and your boss is agreeable, you can also use this time to get some schoolwork done. Just be sure to not jeopardize your job by trying to multitask, as the strain of getting into trouble at work, or worse yet losing your job, is likely to render it even more difficult to focus on your schooling.

Mass transit. If you drive a long distance to and from work, you may be losing many hours each day in productivity. Driving has multiple effects on your day—not only do you lose the time that you actually spend driving, but you are likely to be more tired once you get home as well, rendering it difficult to focus on your studies. Explore the possibility of using mass transit or getting into a ride share program. With mass transit, you can read or rest during your commute, draft written assignments by hand and then type them later, or, if you have a laptop, get some writing done in transit. If your budget supports having a mobile broadband connection, you can actually access your online classroom during your commute.

If you carpool, be realistic about the types of work that you could do while riding in a car with others. It may be difficult to concentrate, or there may be a social expectation that you will engage in conversation during the ride. Still, consider other ways that a ride share could support your schooling. For example, you may be less tired at the end of the day if you are not driving, facilitating your productivity once you are at home. You might also consider setting aside the money that you save on gas for technology upgrades that will support your schooling, such as a new laptop.

Parenting time. Online students who have children at home may find it particularly difficult to make school a priority. Children may not understand the nature or importance of college study, and may be demanding of attention above and beyond their physical needs, making it difficult to focus. It may be necessary to sometimes call on the support of friends or loved ones to assist with child care as you work on major assignments. There are other ways of balancing schoolwork with parenting, though. Instead of reading a standard bedtime story, some students have read assigned textbook readings to their infants in a soothing voice; this allows students to complete his or her readings while also providing the young child the benefit of time with his or her parent. For some children, parents may be successful in hosting "reading time" in which the parent works while the child reads his or her own books, or, for older children, having "family study time," where the parent works on assignments as the child completes homework. Providing some reward for everyone completing their work, such as watching a favorite movie or having ice cream, can provide incentive for the family to stay focused during that time.

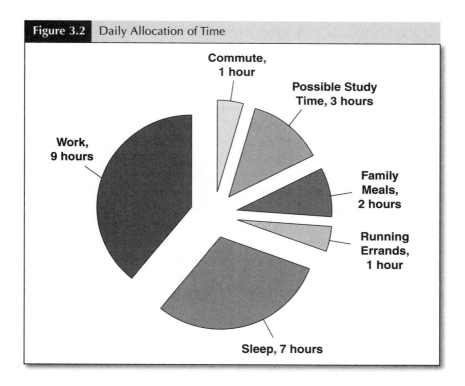

Figure 3.2   Daily Allocation of Time

❖ THE IMPORTANCE OF BALANCE

Working to integrate college into an already-busy schedule can be a challenge. Online coursework may be particularly difficult, as students may not have realized how much time would be required. If your schedule is starting to feel out of control, look more carefully at how you are spending your time to assess whether there is a way to lessen other time commitments. Cook larger batches of food and freeze the leftovers for dinner on another day; combine shopping trips into a single weekly outing; if you work an hourly wage job and can afford to do so, consider asking for a reduction in hours.

As you look for ways to allocate sufficient time to your schooling, don't forget the importance of maintaining balance in your day. While it is easy to get into a trap where you feel that you "don't have time" to go for a walk, indulge in a movie, or go out with friends, failure to take time to relax can actually slow down your work pace, which can turn into a self-fulfilling prophecy. Use short breaks as an incentive to complete your work, and take a nap if you realize that you are having difficulty focusing. It may seem counter-intuitive, but taking breaks and getting enough sleep will actually help you find more time in your day by allowing you to work more efficiently.

> Learning Tip: Make sure that you get enough sleep, as it will ultimately support your productivity.

❖ CONCLUSION

You should now have a better idea of where you might study and how you might balance your schoolwork with other responsibilities. By staying organized and using the tricks provided to "find" time in your day, you can maximize your efficiency when studying and completing assignments. Fully exploit the flexibility of online coursework by reflecting critically on where and when you work the most efficiently and then developing habits that make the most of those spaces and times.

REFLECTION QUESTIONS

1. What characteristics do you look for in a good work environment? Taking these factors into consideration, identify at least three places where you might conduct your schoolwork.

2. Do you think that you could use your time more efficiently, and if so, how? Do you think that you dedicate enough time to your studies?

3. What challenges do you anticipate in maintaining balance while you pursue your degree, and how can you address them?

CHAPTER CHECKLIST

☐ Gather the items that you need to support your studies and place them in a central location ("home base").

☐ Identify viable work areas using the four-step process in this chapter.

☐ If you expect to work away from home on a regular basis, put together an "on-the-road study pack" and compose a checklist of the included items.

☐ Identify how you might make more efficient use of your time throughout your day in a manner that supports your studies.

☐ Establish a weekly schedule that includes dedicated time for studying, resting, and enjoying time with friends or loved ones.

RELATED RESOURCES

Home Office Design	www.hgtv.com/designers-portfolio/home-offices/index.html
Study Tips	www.academictips.org
Study Tips	www.helium.com/knowledge/185414-10-study-tips-for-college-students
Time Management	www.mayoclinic.com/health/time-management/WL00048
Time Management	www.collegeboard.com/student/plan/college-success/118.html

❖ NOTES

1. See page 7 of Davies, R. S. (2003). Learner intent and online courses. *The Journal of Interactive Online Learning, 2*(1), 1–10.

2. Aragon, S. R., Johnson, S. D., & Shaik, N. (2002). The influence of learning style preferences on student success in online versus face-to-face environments. *The American Journal of Distance Education, 16*(4), 227–244.

4

Where Do I Turn for Help?

Knowing Your Resources

❖ INTRODUCTION

As an online student, it can be intimidating to figure out where to turn for help. You may hold the misconception that online learners are supposed to be entirely self-sufficient, navigating the classroom and expectations without any assistance. You may believe that online schools have few resources, or that your instructors will lose respect for you if you ask for help. A couple of important points may go a long way in countering these misconceptions. First, if students were expected to learn on their own, there would be no need for schools! By definition, schools exist to support student learning, so you shouldn't hesitate to take advantage of the resources that are funded by your tuition dollars. Second, needing help is not indicative of failure; it is a part of being human. This may be especially true in the context of your education—you are learning something new, in a new environment, and, if you are like many online students, you are doing so while juggling a number of other responsibilities. This chapter is intended to help you efficiently and effectively navigate the many resources that you may find useful as you work toward your degree.

❖ GETTING ANSWERS TO SCHOOL-SPECIFIC QUESTIONS

You are likely to have a number of questions as you begin your online courses. Most schools assign each student to an "advisor" who serves as a central point of contact for these types of questions. Some schools maintain a staff specifically dedicated to advising, whereas others have professors advise students in addition to their teaching duties. Since your advisor is likely to be familiar with the expectations and policies of your school, he or she will serve as a good general resource when you are unsure of where else to turn. Even if the advisor cannot answer your question directly, he or she is likely to be able to send you in the right direction. Questions that you might bring to your advisor include the following:

- What classes do I have to take, and how do I register for them?
- Do my prior experiences or education qualify me for credits with the school?
- What are the requirements for graduation?
- What resources are available to help me with my studies?
- Where do I turn if I think I have a disability that warrants accommodations?
- What happens if I need some time off in the middle of my schooling?

While you shouldn't hesitate to contact your advisor as needed, you can also empower yourself to find answers to some of your own questions about your degree plan and your school's policies. Most schools publish an *academic catalog* that provides a brief description of each course offered, as well as an account of which courses are required to complete your degree. Academic policies relevant to your education may also be found in the catalog, on the school Web site, or in a student handbook. Read these resources carefully, and take note of policies and requirements that may be relevant to your schooling.

Learning Tip: Make sure that you have a solid understanding of the graduation requirements for your program.

❖ TECHNOLOGICAL RESOURCES

Unlike traditional schools, where those armed with little more than a campus map should be able to make it to class without much difficulty, your attendance in an online class is highly contingent upon technology operating properly. While this may seem intuitive, it is mentioned here to help you navigate the diversity of available technology-related resources. Schools may offer any of a variety of technical support options, but you shouldn't expect to rely entirely upon your school for matters of technology.

School-Based Technical Support

Some schools maintain a central, in-house (school-run) technical support team to assist with questions related to e-mail, the school Web site, the online learning platform, and, for those living on campus, Internet access in the dorms. Other schools may provide a separate technical support number specifically for the online learning platform. Take note of any contact information that you can locate for technical support at your school, including phone numbers, e-mail addresses, or how to access live chat, and post it in a prominent location. If your school offers more than one way of contacting technical support, be thoughtful in selecting the most efficient mechanism for communicating your issue. Non-urgent matters may best be handled by e-mail. Sometimes telephone provides the most efficient way of describing complex issues, but live chat may render it easier to be doing other work if you are put on hold, as you can have other windows open on your computer while you are watching for the technical support specialist to return.

Local Resources

In addition to being familiar with the technical support services provided by your school, you should have contact information on-hand for local businesses that can support you with three types of potential issues:

- *Computer Problems*—Identify a local computer repair shop that is familiar with your brand of computer. Major brands such as

Apple and Toshiba may maintain independent repair shops or offer technical support at their retail stores (as with Apple's "Genius Bar"). You may also be able to locate an independent shop that can provide assistance. When your computer starts to "act up"—when it takes you to an error message on startup, or the mouse stops responding, or some other miscellaneous issue—you will be glad to know where to turn for assistance.

- *Internet Problems*—Add the number for your Internet provider to your contact list. If you are unable to connect to the Internet, calling your provider will help you most efficiently assess whether there is an area-wide outage (for example, due to a storm) or whether you may need a technician to visit your home to fix the problem. Your Internet provider may also be able to walk you through some basic troubleshooting.

- *Data Corruption*—If the repair shop that you identified for computer repair does not specifically offer services in data recovery, find a service that does, and keep their number on-hand as well. You may encounter a situation in which your computer appears to be operating perfectly, but you receive an error message upon trying to open a specific file. An expert in data recovery may be able to recover your work.

Online Resources

For those instances where you encounter difficulty but are still able to access the Internet, there are also a number of online resources available. It is unlikely that you are the first person to encounter a given technical issue, so it may be helpful to enter a description of the problem into a search engine such as Google to see whether anyone else has posted potential "fixes." Some major computer manufacturers also offer online support for their customers:

- Dell: www.support.dell.com

- Toshiba: www.Toshiba.com

- Apple: www.apple.com/support

Not every technical issue can be prevented—some may recall the time that Bill Gates suffered a crash of Windows 98 on live television—but knowing where to turn can help lessen the stress that results.

Learning Tip: Knowing where you can turn when things go wrong can minimize your loss of productivity due to technical issues.

❖ ACADEMIC RESOURCES

Academic resources are those that directly support you in the completion of coursework. Regardless of your school's structure, a good place to start when you run into difficulty with your coursework is your professor—he or she will be the most intimately familiar with the course content and what is expected for any given assignment. If your instructor provides a telephone number or e-mail address, or hosts office hours online or (for those located near a campus) in a physical office, make use of them! If you are concerned about imposing on an instructor's time, simply ask him or her about any limitations to availability to make sure that your contact with the instructor remains within reason. For example, instructors may ask that students not call after a certain time of night, and some may ask that students not contact them on instant messaging outside of their office hours.

School-Based Resources

Since schools understand that their success is predicated on the quality of education that their students receive, they may also provide access to tutors, a writing center or math center, or other forms of study support. There is no reason to struggle alone when your tuition dollars are specifically going toward resources to help you. Some schools have other individuals available to assist students on a one-on-one basis. They may go by names such as "mentor," "tutor," "peer advisor," or "teaching assistant" and may be able to assist with the course content and/or navigating the online school environment. Schools may also offer opportunities to connect with a "study buddy" in your area. If you are struggling with your schoolwork despite your contact with the instructor, or if you feel that you are drawing too heavily upon your instructor's time, find out whether your school offers any additional resources of this type.

Writing or math centers are dedicated to helping students throughout a given school with the development of their math and writing skills. If available, these centers may offer any combination of tutoring, review services (for example, in which the writing center provides feedback on students' written work), or "libraries" of resources (either on-ground or in the form of online documents) to support students in developing these specialized skills. Documents provided may include sample papers, examples of citation styles such as APA or MLA, or down-to-earth explanations of basic writing conventions. Since the resources available are designed to address common challenges encountered by students in these areas, it is worthwhile to take a few minutes early on to find out whether your school has one or both of these centers, and if so, what they offer.

Most schools, even those that operate solely online, will offer some form of library resources. The earlier you learn to navigate them, the better! As outlined in Chapter 8, the library is your key to accessing academic journal articles and other resources that will be necessary for completing research papers. You may also find yourself in need of information for other reasons—for example, you may want to do research to investigate possible career paths, or to support a work project. "Knowledge is power," and the path to knowledge typically runs through the library. Your school may also offer access to librarians via telephone, e-mail, or live chat; if so, don't hesitate to reach out with questions regarding how to navigate the library Web site.

Students who attend schools that do not offer tutoring services or coordinated study groups need not consider themselves "out of luck." If you are located near a campus affiliated with your school, you may be able to meet your classmates at the student union or a local restaurant or coffee shop to study together. Even if your class is geographically dispersed, there are plenty of affordable ways to study "with" your classmates. For example, you might arrange to log into an instant messaging tool at the same time so that you can ask each other questions as you encounter difficulty with your coursework. (See "Social Resources" later in this chapter for additional details on tools for staying in touch.) These types of "study dates" enable students to learn from one another and can also support the maintenance of a disciplined study schedule.

External Sources of Academic Support

There are a number of publicly available services to support online students. For a fee, sites such as www.eduwizards.com, www.tutor.com, and www.smarthinking.com provide students with online tutors in their area of study. Other sites offer free study tools; for example, www.flashcardexchange.com allows users to maintain a free account to create, store, and study with electronic flashcards (with the ability to print for a small fee), and www.studystack.com allows users to create study materials and search through materials created by others.

If you are struggling with a particular topic, consider looking for explanations posted to the Internet by professors from different schools, as it can sometimes be helpful to hear the same material presented in slightly different ways. You may also be able to find video lectures posted to www.youtube.com that break down complex processes or that present theories, inventions, business models, or medical advancements straight from the mouths of those who created them.

There are also a number of resources specifically targeted toward students who need assistance with their writing. You might consider investing in books such as Diane Hacker's *Rules for Writers* or William Strunk Jr. and E. B. White's *The Elements of Style*. The writing lab at Purdue University is also a well-respected resource: http://owl.english.purdue.edu/.

❖ SOCIAL RESOURCES

College is often thought to be a social as well as an academic experience. Those who take classes online may initially fear that they will be isolated or lack the sense of intellectual community that is present on college campuses. In fact, the social nature of "college life" is not lacking for online learners; many schools have invested in significant resources in building a sense of community among online students.

School-Based Resources

Schools may offer social networks or instant messaging tools available only to students, host social gathering areas within each classroom that are designated as a "student lounge," "coffee shop," or "virtual café," or organize student clubs akin to (and often affiliated with) those that would exist at brick-and-mortar campuses. Some schools have even hosted online book clubs and recipe clubs in efforts to build a "virtual community" among their students.[1]

Publicly Available Resources

For those who find themselves yearning for more social interaction than their school provides, there are a number of public resources available to facilitate support systems among geographically dispersed classmates.

Instant Messaging (IM) tools. These tools allow students to create a user profile, view others that are online, and engage in real-time written chat with those individuals.[2] While some schools may host their own instant messaging tools, other free and publicly available services include Yahoo Messenger, MSN Instant Messenger, AOL Instant Messenger (AIM), and Google Talk. Some of these tools, such as Google Talk, offer more robust communication capabilities such as voice calls or video chat over the Internet. These tools can provide students with a much-needed real-time support system. In one study, while students reported chatting through instant messaging, others "commented on how comforting it was to be working on a paper and to just see other students online with their IM connection . . . a certain sense of community was often conveyed by IM without any interaction at all."[3]

Social networking sites. These sites host "member-based Internet communities"[4] that facilitate the interaction of members through a number of mechanisms including profiles, blog-type tools, photo-sharing, and both synchronous and asynchronous communication capabilities. Facebook and MySpace are perhaps the best-known social networking sites, though other options include "Friendster, LiveJournal, and Bebo."[5] These sites provide a good platform for staying in contact with current and past classmates.

Internet telephone services. There are a number of services that allow users to make free or low-cost voice and video calls over the Internet. These services provide an affordable alternative if your phone plan does not include unlimited long distance; they are often less expensive than making frequent long-distance calls on a traditional phone line or risking an overage of minutes on a cell phone. Services such as Skype and Logitech Vid specialize in computer-to-computer video and audio calls that operate with microphones and webcams. These services are useful for connecting easily to others who spend a significant amount of time at their computers. "Voice over Internet Protocol" (VoIP) services such as Vonage and MagicJack allow users to connect their standard phone through their Internet connection with the use of a router or adapter; for the most part, calls therefore resemble traditional telephone services, though the audio is transmitted via the Internet rather than a traditional phone line.

❖ COUNSELING SERVICES

At some point in your schooling, you may find that you need assistance beyond what your social support system can provide. Whether you are one of the more than 57 million adults in the United States

Figure 4.1 A Sample Facebook Page

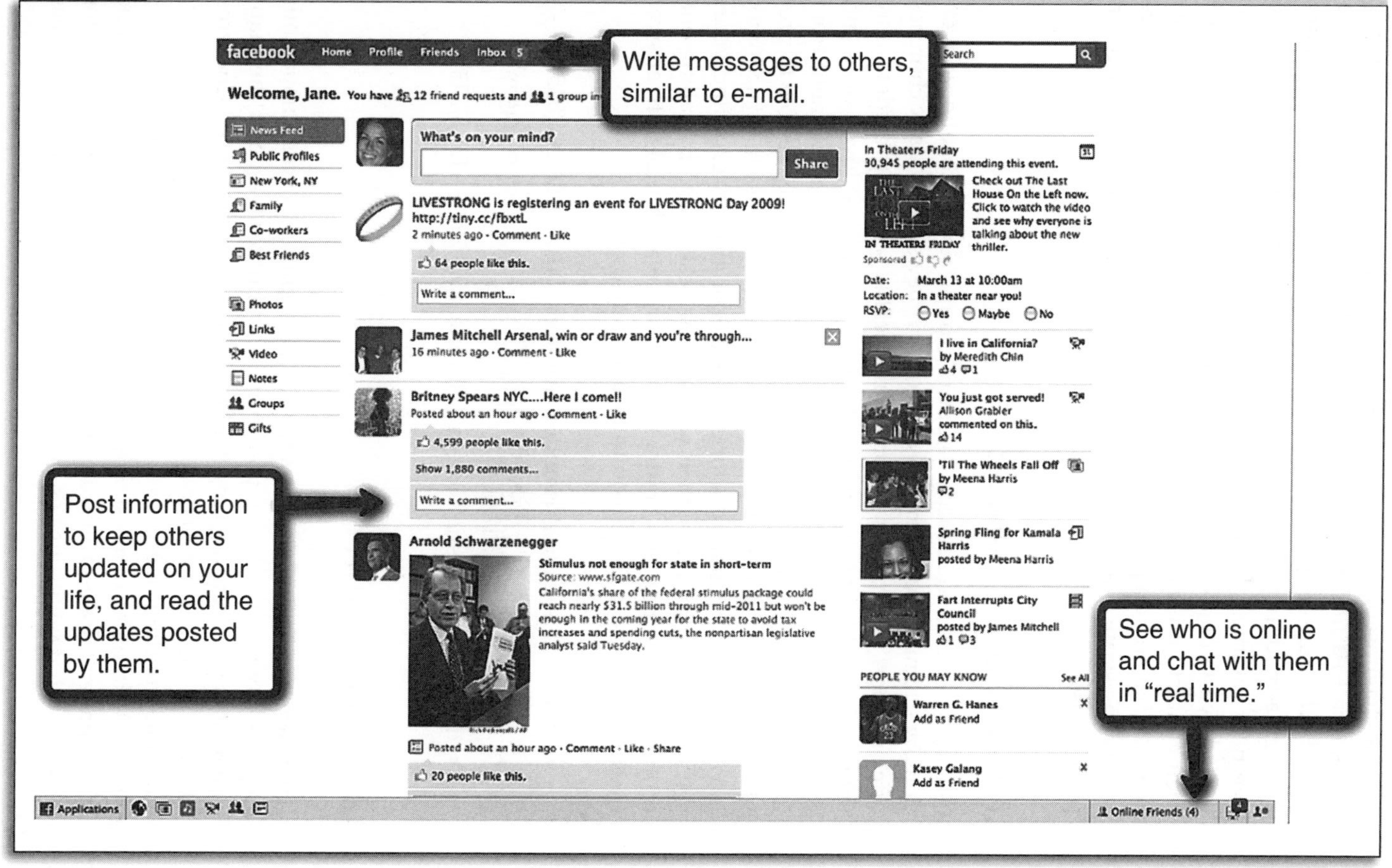

Write messages to others, similar to e-mail.

See who is online and chat with them in "real time."

Post information to keep others updated on your life, and read the updates posted by them.

facebook   Home Profile Friends Inbox 5

Welcome, Jane. You have 12 friend requests and 1 group in

News Feed

Public Profiles

New York, NY
Family
Co-workers
Best Friends

Photos
Links
Video
Notes
Groups
Gifts

What's on your mind?

Share

LIVESTRONG is registering an event for LIVESTRONG Day 2009!
http://tiny.cc/fbxtl
2 minutes ago · Comment · Like

64 people like this.

Write a comment...

James Mitchell Arsenal, win or draw and you're through...
16 minutes ago · Comment · Like

Britney Spears NYC....Here I come!!
Posted about an hour ago · Comment · Like

4,599 people like this.

Show 1,880 comments...

Write a comment...

Arnold Schwarzenegger

Stimulus not enough for state in short-term
Source: www.sfgate.com
California's share of the federal stimulus package could
reach nearly $31.5 billion through mid-2011 but won't be
enough in the coming year for the state to avoid tax
increases and spending cuts, the nonpartisan legislative
analyst said Tuesday.

Posted about an hour ago · Comment · Like · Share

20 people like this.

Search

In Theaters Friday
30,945 people are attending this event.

Check out The Last
House On the Left now.
Click to watch the video
and see why everyone is
talking about the new
thriller.

IN THEATERS FRIDAY

Sponsored

Date: March 13 at 10:00am
Location: In a theater near you!
RSVP: Yes   Maybe   No

I live in California?
by Meredith Chin
4 1

You just got served!
Allison Grabler
commented on this.
14

'Til The Wheels Fall Off
by Meena Harris
2

Spring Fling for Kamala
Harris
posted by Meena Harris

Fart Interrupts City
Council
posted by James Mitchell
1 3

PEOPLE YOU MAY KNOW   See All

Warren G. Hanes
Add as Friend

Kasey Galang
Add as Friend

Applications

Online Friends (4)

with a diagnosable mental illness[6] or you are simply experiencing stress due to a life change or the extent of your responsibilities, you may find counseling beneficial. If you are taking online classes through a predominantly brick-and-mortar institution and happen to live near campus, you are likely to be in luck—most traditional colleges have strong counseling services. You should be able to locate their contact information by doing a search on your school's Web site. Schools that are run predominantly online are much less likely to have counseling services available, but there are plenty of other resources in place to assist.

Publicly Available Resources

You may be able to identify support groups run by local organizations by scanning the "events" section of your newspaper. Many churches offer support groups for divorce, and health service providers may sponsor bereavement groups for those who have lost loved ones and those facing serious illness. If you believe that you could benefit from individual therapy, then your primary care doctor may be able to provide you with a referral. If you are unsure of where else to turn, do not have access to a primary doctor due to lack of insurance, or find yourself in a moment of crisis, then you may be best served by calling one of the following national hotlines, which are available 24/7 to answer questions or help connect you to local resources:

- National Suicide Prevention Lifeline: 800–273-TALK (8255)

- National Substance Abuse Hotline: 800–662-HELP (4357)

- National Domestic Violence Hotline: 800–799-SAFE (7233)

❖ FINANCIAL SUPPORT

There are two financial aspects worthy of attention as you pursue your degree—how you will pay your tuition and other fees, and the management of your general budget as it relates to those expenses. Concerns about how to pay for schooling are common. Luckily, a number of potential funding sources exist to help. Your school should have a financial aid office to assist with navigating potential funding sources. If you haven't done so already, you should complete the application for student aid at www.fafsa.ed.gov; this application is required to access funding from the federal government, but may also be used by your state or college to allocate funds.[7]

As you figure out how to pay for your schooling, it may be helpful to understand the different types of funding available. Some forms of support need to be repaid, while others do not. Some are based on financial need, while others are not.

- Scholarships
- Grants
- Loans
- Other types of funding

Scholarships. Even if you are fortunate enough to pay for school from personal savings, it may be worthwhile to explore scholarships to offset your school-related expenses. Scholarships are typically based on criteria other than financial need, such as membership in a particular group (ranging from being the child of a military veteran, to those working in, or planning to study in, a particular industry) or performance in an essay competition, and do not need to be repaid if you fulfill the conditions set forth by the sponsor.[8] The federal government maintains a searchable database of scholarships at www.studentaid2.ed.gov/getmoney/scholarship/v3browse.asp. You may also want to explore whether your school hosts any internal scholarship competitions.

Grants. For students who are concerned about their ability to pay for schooling, grants may be a solution. Similar to scholarships, grants usually do not need to be repaid, but they are usually allocated, at least in part, based on the financial need of the recipient.[9]

Loans. Loans are probably the easiest source of funding to obtain for college, but they need to be paid back after a certain amount of time along with interest. The federal government coordinates the issuance of certain types of loans and, in some cases, will "subsidize" (offset some of the interest on) loans but students will ultimately be responsible for repayments. Loans are also available through private lenders, such as local banks. Loans can be a viable source of funding if you don't possess the resources to pay for your schooling outright but you anticipate having the earning potential to be able to make payments when the loans come due. Loans are not "free money," so it is important to explore the interest rate and other terms of repayment and consider their impact on your household finances. Still, if you are committed to earning your degree, the financial commitment is likely to prove worthwhile.

Other types of funding. Depending upon your life situation, you may be able to access other sources of funding. If you are currently working, your employer may offer tuition reimbursement. Funding is also available for veterans and active members of the military. Take the time to explore all sources of financing; the more support you can secure, the better!

Managing Your Household Finances

Unless you are one of the few students who are fortunate enough to receive a "free ride" through scholarships and grants, your schooling will have some impact on your household finances. If you pay outright, it may still be helpful to budget or increase your income to compensate for the expenses. If you receive loans that cover your school-related expenses, maintain control of your finances so that you are in a position to make payments once they are due. For all of the financial advice that bombards us through books, television shows, and online articles, there are only two ways for anyone, rich or poor, to improve their financial situation:

1. Reduce spending

2. Increase income

There will be a lot of variation in how you carry out these steps depending upon your specific financial circumstances. If you are struggling financially and already working to your full earnings potential, you will need to find ways to decrease your expenses. Steps that can be taken range from the small to the large; anything from canceling your daily trip to the coffee shop to moving to a place with lower rent can help. Some other ideas for saving money while minimally compromising your quality of life include the following:

- Buy books, clothes, electronics, and other household items through resale shops or Web sites instead of new.

- Use generic versions of your favorite products.

- Cook instead of eating at restaurants, and buy groceries based on what is on sale. (If time is a constraint, consider cooking in bulk so that you can simply reheat meals.)

- Comparison-shop, especially for major purchases.

Take some time to evaluate your current employment situation and consider whether you may either be over-employed or under-employed as you embark on your schooling. If you are not currently working, you may find that taking on a part-time job adds structure to your week, and the extra income may help you pay for incidentals or build your savings to repay loans. If you are currently working long hours, it may be worthwhile to reflect on whether you can afford to cut back in order to dedicate more time to your schooling.

❖ CONCLUSION

With so many resources available to support college students, there is no reason for you to feel as though you are "going it alone." Your school provides services that exist specifically to support student success. There are also many publicly available resources that you may find helpful. Take full advantage of what is available.

REFLECTION QUESTIONS

1. Which of the social tools listed in this chapter do you already use? Which tools do you want to use to stay in touch with classmates, if any?

2. Do you have concerns about funding your education? Brainstorm about steps that you can take to improve your financial situation.

CHAPTER CHECKLIST

☐ Locate and skim the policies in your school's academic catalog and/or student handbook.

☐ Make a list of any questions that you have regarding your degree plan, and contact your advisor with those questions.

☐ Write down the telephone numbers for:
  • Your academic advisor
  • Technical support (both school and local resources)

☐ Research and list the academic support services provided by your school.

☐ Create a monthly budget that will help you manage your finances while in school.

RELATED RESOURCES

Academic Support

Free Study Aids	www.flashcardexchange.com
Free Study Aids	www.studystack.com
Free Study Aids	www.youtube.com
Online Tutors (Fee-Based)	www.eduwizards.com
Online Tutors (Fee-Based)	www.tutor.com
Online Tutors (Fee-Based)	www.smarthinking.com

Computer Support

Apple Computers	www.apple.com/support
Compaq Computers	www.compaq.com/country/cpq_support.html
Dell Computers	www.support.dell.com
Gateway Computers	http://support.gateway.com/support/cs_post_purcha se.asp
HP Computers	www.hp.com/#Support
Sony Computers	http://esupport.sony.com
Toshiba Computers	www.toshiba.com/tai/support/support_cons.jsp

Personal Support

Domestic Violence	www.ndvh.org (800–799–7233)
Financial—Application for Financial Aid	www.fafsa.ed.gov
Financial—Searchable Scholarship Database	www.studentaid2.ed.gov/getmoney/ scholarship/v3browse.asp
Substance Abuse and Mental Health	www.samhsa.gov/treatment/index.a spx (800–662–4357)
Suicide Prevention	www.suicidepreventionlifeline.org (800–273–8255)

Social Tools

Computer-to-Computer Video Calling	Skype www.skype.com
Computer-to-Computer Video Calling	Logitech Vid www.logitech.com/index.cfm/home/&cl=us,en
Internet Phone Plan (VoIP)	MagicJack www.magicjack.com
Internet Phone Plan (VoIP)	Vonage www.vonage.com
Live Chat	AOL Instant Messenger (AIM) http://dashboard.aim.com/aim
Live Chat	MSN Instant Messenger http://download.live.com/messenger
Live Chat with Video Calling Capability	Google Talk www.google.com/talk
Live Chat with Video Calling Capability	Yahoo Messenger http://messenger.yahoo.com
Social Networking Site	Bebo www.bebo.com
Social Networking Site	Facebook www.facebook.com
Social Networking Site	Friendster www.friendster.com
Social Networking/Blog Site	LiveJournal www.livejournal.com
Social Networking/Blog Site	MySpace www.myspace.com

Writing Help

Citations/General Help	http://owl.english.purdue.edu
Dictionary	www.dictionary.com
Thesaurus	www.thesaurus.com

❖ NOTES

1. Battista, L., Forrey, C., & Stevenson, C. (2008). It takes a virtual community: Promoting collaboration through student activities. *Online Journal of Distance Learning Administration, 11*(2), retrieved from http://www.westga.edu/~distance/ojdla/summer112/battista112.html

2. Kadirire, J. (2007). Instant messaging for creating interactive and collaborative m-learning environments. *International Review of Research in Open and Distance Learning, 8*(2), 1–14.

3. See page 270 of Sparks, P. (2006). Electronic note passing: Enriching online learning with new communications tools. *MERLOT Journal of Online Learning and Teaching, 2*(4), 268–274.

4. See page 227 of Pempek, T. A., Yevdokiya, A. Y., & Calvert, S. L. (2009). College students' social networking experiences on Facebook. *Journal of Applied Developmental Psychology, 30*, 227–238.

5. See page 227 of Pempek, T. A., Yevdokiya, A. Y., & Calvert, S. L. (2009). College students' social networking experiences on Facebook. *Journal of Applied Developmental Psychology, 30*, 227–238.

6. National Institute of Mental Health, 2009.

7. Federal Student Aid. (2009). Student aid on the Web. Funding Your Education. Retrieved from http://studentaid.ed.gov.

8. U.S. Department of Education. (2009). How to pay. "I'm Going" Guide. Retrieved from http://www.college.gov/wps/portal

9. U.S. Department of Education. (2009). How to pay. "I'm Going" Guide. Retrieved from http://www.college.gov/wps/portal

5

When the Worst Happens and How to Cope

❖ INTRODUCTION

This chapter begins with what may seem to be a negative initial message: In spite of the best planning, things can, and likely will, go wrong at some point in your schooling. The Internet goes down, files are corrupted, or personal issues arise unexpectedly. Still, this chapter does not tell a story of defeat; rather, it acknowledges that life does not always go as planned, and it equips readers with practical tips for preventing, minimizing the impact of, and responding most effectively to stressful situations.

❖ THE IMPORTANCE OF PERSPECTIVE

As you read through this chapter, keep in mind that you can't always control your circumstances, but you do control how you respond to them. You enrolled in your program of study for a reason. Never lose sight of the end-goal. When you fall on hard times, focus on what needs to be done to accomplish the goals that you have set for yourself. When you look back on your schooling in a few years, consider what you want your story to be. Crises that seem insurmountable now will turn into memories that range from the humorous to the inspiring.

Sometimes everything seems to go wrong, but time will add perspective if you persevere. Plenty of college graduates who have taken online courses can reflect on stories such as the time that their Internet connection had faltered just prior to a deadline, forcing them to venture into the darkness of night to frantically search for an open coffee shop or other "hot spot" to submit their work—only to have an emotional breakdown on the side of the road after suffering a flat tire. Even if a student in this situation were to submit their work a day late, the worst that would likely come of it would be a late penalty; as stressful as such a situation might be, it does not spell disaster for a person's lifelong academic goals! It can be helpful to maintain perspective during such stressful situations, and maybe even find some humor in their absurdity.

Other college graduates can reflect on more somber struggles, in which they fought a life-threatening illness, recovered from a serious accident, or oversaw their parents' end-of-life care while also working to complete their degree. Such situations are incredibly difficult, but students may find motivation to persevere due to their own lifelong goals, the wishes of their loved ones, or their desire to serve as an inspiration for others who may fall on difficult times. Others may welcome their schoolwork as a mental "break" from the other stressors that they are facing in their life. As you read this chapter, take note of the tips for best handling these types of major life stressors while still working toward your academic goals.

❖ TECHNOLOGY MATTERS

Online students undoubtedly form a love/hate relationship with technology. Advancements in technology have allowed some to access a college education who might otherwise have been unable, bringing college to the living room in a more engaging manner than old correspondence courses. Technology contributes to efficiency; most students would lament having to complete their schoolwork by hand or on a typewriter, as computers make it far easier to save and edit work. Online learning tools have become more advanced and user-friendly with time, and as instructors gain comfort with technology, many are beginning to experiment with interactive or multimedia tools. Thank goodness for technology!

Unfortunately, technology is imperfect. While it is common to think of computer issues as anomalous events, expecting a computer to run without problems is analogous to thinking that a person can exist without suffering any ailments, or that a car can keep running indefinitely without mechanical problems. Even the most reliable computer is fallible. Many students have experienced sitting at their computer, admiring the near-genius paper that has just been completed, when the screen suddenly goes blank, or the word processor inexplicably shuts down, or something else goes horribly awry. This knowledge alone will not "take off the edge" when these experiences actually happen, but it may help to know that you are not alone in such stressful situations, and help you gain perspective as you prepare to best respond to them.

❖ TIPS AND TRICKS TO MINIMIZE TECHNICAL CATASTROPHES

In addition to the basic computer set-up that was addressed in Chapter 2—ensuring that you have installed virus protection and all of the programs necessary to interact with your school's online platform—there are some additional steps that can be taken to minimize potentially stressful technological situations. All of the recommendations listed here involve different ways of backing up your work. In situations in which a file becomes unrecoverable due to some technological issue, or in which work that was typed into a field on a discussion board or in e-mail is lost, the greatest gift that you can give yourself is the knowledge that you have another copy of that work saved somewhere. There are three central strategies for backing up your work:

- Adjust your word processor settings
- Manually back up your work
- Draft your discussion board contributions in a word processing file

Adjust Your Word Processor Settings

Most word processing software has a setting that determines how frequently your computer backs up your document as you work. Use the "help" feature of your software to investigate whether you can adjust the "document recovery" settings to back up your work frequently.

You should still save your work manually, but changing the document recovery settings will minimize the loss of work if the program closes unexpectedly or your computer shuts down while you are working. If your word processor is set to auto-save every 60 minutes, then you may lose as much as 60 minutes of work if your program closes unexpectedly and you have not yet saved your changes. If your word processor is set to auto-save every 5 minutes, then you are unlikely to lose more than 5 minutes of work when the same thing happens—a truly beautiful thing!

Figure 5.1   Screen Shot of How to Adjust Auto Save Setting

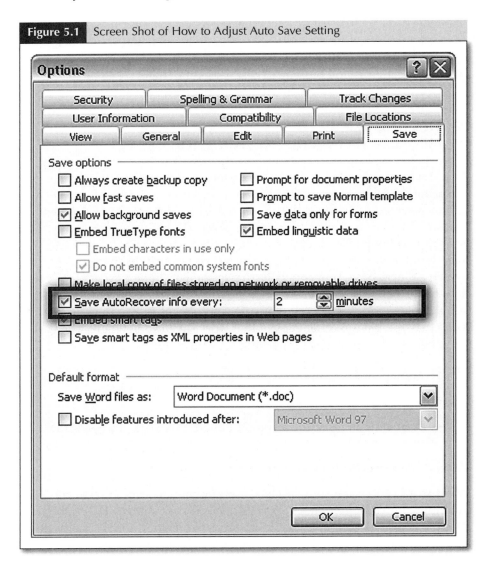

Manually Back Up Your Work

Even when you have taken all of the necessary precautions, there is still the risk of some "fatal flaw" resulting in the corruption and subsequent loss of your files. In order to minimize the risk of losing your work, get into the practice of keeping a backup drive (either a flash drive or, for the more technologically inclined, a backup hard drive) and saving all files on both your computer and the additional drive every time you work. It is easy to lose diligence with such practices, so try to keep the external drive near your computer or in your laptop bag and make it a habit to copy all of your newly edited files to the drive each day before you shut down. If you have not yet purchased a flash drive, improvise by sending a copy of your work to your own e-mail address or storing a backup copy online with a free service such as Google Docs.

Draft Your Discussion Board
Contributions in a Word Processing File

In most online platforms, there is at least some risk of losing discussion contributions when you attempt to post them. You may receive an error message that your session has "timed out," or you may be booted back to your school's login screen or find out that you have lost your Internet connection entirely. As students sometimes spend a great deal of time crafting their discussion board postings, it is worthwhile to develop work habits that minimize the risk of such loss. One mechanism for doing so is to draft responses in a word processing document, and then cut and paste it into the proper field in the classroom. On most computer systems, to copy, use your mouse to select the relevant text, and hold the "Control" or "Command" button as you also hit "C." To paste, use your mouse to click into the field where you would like the text to appear, and hold down the "Control" or "Command" button as you also hit "V." This technique will minimize the risk of losing your work before it has been posted, since you would still have your work in the word processing document.

> *Learning Tip: Back up your files frequently to minimize the risk of losing your work.*

❖ RESPONDING TO COMMON PROBLEMS

Even with the best planning, a top-of-the-line computer, a high speed Internet connection, and all compatible programs downloaded, things will occasionally go wrong. The general advice for such situations is to (1) use your resources and (2) step into action. Some students get angry when things don't go smoothly. Others get depressed, and many simply feel overwhelmed. It can be easy to get carried away in the emotions of the moment, and it is important to find outlets for those emotions—venting to a friend or fellow student, or taking a short break to listen to music, go for a walk, or simply breathe deeply. Still, the goal of these short breaks should ultimately be to work through the emotions so that you can refocus your energy where it needs to be—on bouncing back from the setback. The following is additional guidance on common issues faced by online learners.

You tried to post a discussion comment/submit an assignment and encountered an error message. If you have time before the deadline and your school provides technical support, call them for assistance. If your school does not offer technical support or a deadline is looming, notify your instructor of the issue immediately. If you have a copy of the work that you were trying to submit, e-mail it to the instructor to document that the work was in fact completed. If your work was lost, take a few moments to breathe deeply, and then get started on rewriting it; type in a word processing document even if what you were working on had been a discussion board posting, and save frequently. You can copy and paste the information into the classroom once it is complete; having the work saved, though, will prevent you from having to write it for a third time.

You click onto your Web browser and can't seem to connect to the Internet. First, check to see whether it appears to be an Internet issue or an issue with the specific Web site that you are trying to access. For example, if your school's Web site does not load, try visiting a couple of other sites (such as a news site, or www.google.com) to see if they appear. If they do not, then the issue is likely your Internet connection. To troubleshoot, check to make sure that all lines are plugged in securely; for a wireless connection, try resetting the connection by unplugging the router, letting it sit for a few minutes, and then plugging it back in. If this does not restore the Internet connection, call your Internet provider; even high speed connections will sometimes "go down" (experience temporary disruptions to service).

If everything loads except for a particular site, then the issue is not likely the Internet connection, but rather something on the side of those hosting the site. In this case, simply try again later, or, if you were signing in to address an impending deadline or attend a synchronous meeting, work to make contact with someone from your school, such as technical support or your instructor, to ensure that your issues are documented.

When you start your computer, it brings you directly to a page with an error message. There may be a problem with your computer—either the hardware or your operating system. Try to restart your computer to see whether the error resolves itself. If that doesn't work, take note of the specific error message and call someone who has knowledge of computers, such as a local computer support specialist. Tell them about the error, and get their advice regarding how to proceed.

When things go wrong, if you are unsure of what else to do, call technical support or your local computer specialist to find out what needs to be done to move forward. If your computer is temporarily unusable, come up with a game plan—do you need to ask a friend to use his or her computer for an evening? Some other possible "plan B" options to explore for emergency/temporary computer access are as follows:

- If you live near your school's campus, visit their computer lab.

- Other nearby colleges or universities may allow public access to their computer labs. While typically access is restricted to current students or staff, some colleges allow the general public to pay a small fee to access the lab.

- Public libraries commonly have computers set up for use by their patrons. These public computers can typically be accessed free of charge.

- Various business centers such as FedEx Office may offer computer access to their customers. Just be prepared to pay a fee (by the minute or some other time increment) to use them.

- Some job centers may offer computer access to support community members in their education. Since these centers may give priority to those who are actively working on a resume and conducting a job search, it may be a good idea to call ahead to see whether they would allow you to use their resources for school. This should only be a temporary work-around as you work to fix your computer.

If work was lost and is unrecoverable, start re-creating it. As frustrating as the situation is, the work will not rewrite itself, and instructors cannot grant credit for what they haven't received. The best way to recover is to just keep moving forward.

> *Learning Tip: Always have a backup plan in place for your schoolwork in case you run into technical issues.*

❖ FAMILY, WORK, OR PERSONAL EMERGENCIES

Unfortunately, at some point in their schooling, many students encounter personal crises ranging from accident to illness to a family emergency. Since these events are extremely stressful and often unexpected, it can be easy to feel overwhelmed and become distracted. Students may hesitate to contact their instructors regarding missed deadlines out of fear that they will be viewed as irresponsible, or simply because they are feeling too overwhelmed to deal with their schooling.

It is entirely human to feel overwhelmed when personal crises occur. Still, for those who have made substantial investments of time, money, and effort into earning their degree, and those for whom earning a college degree has great personal and professional significance, simply dropping out or turning a blind eye toward schoolwork should not be an option. There are plenty of possible ways to give personal matters the attention that they warrant without giving up on school or jeopardizing your GPA.

The first step should always be to reach out to your instructor(s) to inform them of your situation. Let them know how much time you feel that you will need before you can look at your schoolwork again, and inquire as to whether they are willing to grant a reasonable extension. If you are far enough into the term that it is not possible to drop the course for a refund, it can only help to explore whether the instructor is willing to work with you. Communication is key in online courses! Whether or not they grant an extension, most online instructors understand that "life happens," and they would much rather hear from you right away than have you contact them after you are too far behind to reasonably get caught up. Receiving an extension of even a few days can help you address the immediate demands of your personal crisis

Figure 5.2	Types of Challenges College Students Experience
Circumstance	**Percentage of Undergraduate Students**
Working Full Time While Enrolled	37.8%
Single Parent	13.3%
Reported Disability/Difficulty	9.3%

Source: Horn, L., Peter, K., Rooney, K., & Malizio, A. G. (2002). *Profile of Undergraduates in U.S. Postsecondary Institutions: 1999–2000: Statistical Analysis Report.* National Center for Education Statistics: Washington, D.C. http://nces.ed.gov/pubs2002/2002168.PDF

and give you enough time to begin to gain perspective and work on building a support system to ease you through your difficult circumstances. Communication, communication, communication.

If your situation is so overwhelming that you feel fairly certain that you will be unable to complete the term, the next step should be to reach out to your academic advisor or other school contact to assess your options within the school's policies. There is a chance that your school has a mechanism in place to allow students to take some time off from school without adverse consequence. Your school contact should be able to inform you of whether you can still drop a class and with what consequences, or whether you can retake the course later for a higher grade. Securing this information shouldn't take more than a few phone calls, and it can lend peace of mind to know your options for continuing with your education.

❖ PHYSICAL LIMITATIONS TO WRITING

Sometimes online students will encounter personal circumstances that, while not so overwhelming that they feel the need to drop out, will physically preclude their ability to sit at a computer for long periods of time. They may need to undergo arm or hand surgery, or suffer some accident or ailment that impacts normal computer use. While this type of challenge can be quite disheartening at the onset, there are a number of possible work-arounds that can facilitate ongoing involvement in online courses despite these physical limitations. If typing is possible for short periods of time, the solution may be one of time management; you should carve out a number of small pockets of time in which work might be completed so that you can accomplish your academic goals without further aggravating the relevant physical condition.

For those who are rendered entirely unable to sit at a computer, they should arrange to print as many materials as possible so that they can complete their readings and think through assignments while "offline," whether it be in a hospital bed or lying on their couch. Since most of the assignments in online courses must ultimately find their way into type, if you find yourself unable to type you will need to tap either social or technological resources to facilitate your ongoing success. If you have supportive friends or family members who can spare the time, you might ask those individuals to type as you dictate responses to discussion board postings or other assignments.

Those who are not so fortunate as to have such accommodating friends or relatives, or those who are uncomfortable relying so heavily upon others, should explore the latest in voice recognition technology. Programs such as Dragon NaturallySpeaking convert the users' spoken words into written text. Users dictate into a microphone—some computers have these built in, whereas others will necessitate that students purchase and plug in a headset with microphone—and their words appear in a word processor or other compatible program. Those who can't sit at a computer can sit or lie nearby as they dictate, so long as they are within range of the microphone.

Voice-recognition software may be best suited for those who intend to use it for an extended period of time. In addition to the financial cost, these programs usually require time to be "trained" to the voice of the user. This process involves speaking assigned phrases into the microphone to allow the program to adjust to the user's accent/inflections. Voice-recognition software may also be a solution for those who are simply slow typists, or those who spend enough time online to have concerns about aggravating conditions such as carpal tunnel syndrome.

❖ SCHOOL-RELATED PROBLEMS

As with any social environment, problems may occasionally crop up within the online classroom. Given the amount of interactions that take place, there may be circumstances in which you notice inappropriate contributions by another student, or errors or conflicting information posted by the instructor. If you are concerned about any aspect of the online classroom, your first step should be to contact the instructor in a respectful manner. Many instructors specifically pursue employment with online education because they enjoy interactions with students, and they are typically quite adept at handling student conflicts and other issues. If they are unable to help, they will usually be situated to escalate the issue to someone who is better equipped to do so.

In rare circumstances, you may encounter an instructor who becomes non-responsive, or you may develop concerns about instructors' communications or grading practices, rendering it uncomfortable to approach them directly. In such situations, it may be best to reach out to your academic advisor or other school contact for advice regarding how to proceed. The classroom may also contain tips for escalating concerns, or contact information for an academic chair or other individual situated to assist. If an instructor has truly acted inappropriately or become non-responsive, the school administration will welcome the notification so that they can address the situation.

Please note that sending concerns to fellow classmates in a mass e-mail is not likely to effectively resolve the issue at hand, as it does not bring the concerns to the attention of those with the power to resolve them. School administrators are there to help, and it may be frustrating for them to learn that students have been complaining about an issue for weeks among themselves, but that nobody escalated the issue so that it might be addressed by the school.

> *Learning Tip: If there is a problem in the classroom, notify the instructor or a school administrator immediately.*

❖ WHEN YOU HAVE FALLEN BEHIND . . .

Students may sometimes find that they have temporarily let their circumstances get the best of them, and that they have already missed deadlines as a result. No matter how difficult, the first step in this situation should be to reach out to your instructor. While some students may feel sheepish about contacting their instructor "after the fact," it is best to make contact sooner rather than later to see whether they may be willing to accept late work, and if not, to get their advice regarding where to focus energy. There may be some cases where it is possible to be successful in the class even if a few assignments have been missed. The sooner you can jump back into your coursework, the more likely success will be. If you are feeling particularly overwhelmed, it may also help to identify the assignments that have the greatest allocation of points and to focus your attention on those assignments.

> *Learning Tip: Good communication will be the key to your success. If you are falling behind, reach out to your instructor immediately to discuss the situation.*

❖ CONCLUSION

After reading this chapter, you should feel more comfortable with how to minimize the likelihood of technological catastrophes. You should also feel better equipped to respond to both technological and personal crises as they arise. In most cases, communication with the instructor should be your first step; if you are ever uncertain regarding how to proceed, your academic advisor or other school contact will be able to assist. Above all else, as you encounter difficult circumstances, keep in mind that "this too shall pass." If obtaining your degree has important personal or professional significance, there are few circumstances that would necessitate giving up on your ambitions. Simply work to address issues one step at a time and don't hesitate to turn to your instructor and other support systems for assistance.

REFLECTION QUESTIONS

1. What is the most difficult circumstance that you have ever overcome? How can you apply what you learned in that situation to your schooling?

2. What inspires you to reach your academic goals?

CHAPTER CHECKLIST

☐ Adjust your word processor settings to auto-save frequently.

☐ Secure a flash drive or hard drive, and place it near your computer.

☐ Identify at least two backup options for accessing a computer to complete your schoolwork if you encounter computer/Internet issues.

☐ Develop a communications plan for emergency situations—who would you need to contact at your school if you run into issues, and what is their contact information?

RELATED RESOURCES

Online Document Storage and Collaboration	http://docs.google.com
Voice Recognition Software	www.nuance.com/naturallyspeaking

6

Learning Styles

❖ INTRODUCTION

No two students learn in exactly the same way. Instructors in traditional face-to-face classes are limited in the extent to which they can tailor instruction to individual learning styles. By contrast, in an online environment, students have more control over their navigation of each lesson, providing greater potential for instructors to post information in more than one format to best meet individual student needs. The increased flexibility also supports students' ability to adapt their study habits to the ways in which they prefer to process information. This chapter aims to provide a framework for thinking about your strengths, sensory preferences, and thought processes to best equip you to make the most of your schooling.

❖ KNOW YOUR STRENGTHS

Whether it was a foreign language, business concept, or type of sport, you can probably think of a time that you were able to learn something more easily than other people, or more easily than you have been able to learn other topics or skills. You may think that some of your strong suits are irrelevant to your schooling—for example, it may not be clear how being a good salsa dancer would be relevant to the pursuit of a degree in nursing or information technology. Still, each of your strengths can tell you something about yourself and invariably can help guide you in most effectively approaching your studies.

Multiple Intelligences Theory

There have likely been times in your past that you approached a new task with some amount of fear or uncertainty only to find that with some time and effort you were able to become competent, or even "expert," at that task. The take-away from these experiences is that while not everything will come to you naturally, you *are* capable of learning. These experiences may also provide insights into where your natural strengths are, giving you insights that will help you approach your studies most efficiently.

While everyone is capable of learning, different people vary in where their strengths lie. This has led experts to critique the traditional notion of "intelligence quotient" (IQ) as overly simplistic. A dancer may easily learn a new routine, whereas a nuclear physicist may be quite awkward on the dance floor; another individual may struggle with mathematical concepts but possess the ability to effortlessly compose new songs. In his famous work on multiple intelligences, Howard Gardner[1] accounts for this individual variation in strengths by proposing eight different "intelligence" scales on which people might vary:

- Musical
- Bodily-Kinesthetic
- Logical-Mathematical
- Linguistic
- Spatial
- Interpersonal
- Intrapersonal
- Naturalist

According to Gardner, those who rank high in "bodily-kinesthetic intelligence" possess the ability to use their body to express emotion engage in other activities with a greater ease of skill than others,[2] those with "interpersonal intelligence" more easily pick up on the different moods, temperaments, motivations, and intentions" of others,[3] and so on. All students tend to be strong in at least one of these areas, with some possessing more than one form of intelligence at a high level.

Using Your Intelligence

You may already see connections between items on Gardner's list of intelligences and your selected field of study. Students often pursue an area of study that fits well with their talents. If you have a high level of musical capability, you may pursue a degree in the arts; if you have a natural affinity for understanding ecological systems—an indication of "naturalist intelligence"—you may find that you have chosen to pursue a degree related to natural sciences. Those with a high level of interpersonal intelligence may find themselves in social work or psychology.

Even if you do not see a direct connection between your strongest "intelligences" and your degree plan, you can benefit from letting your natural talents shape your study habits. If you have strong musical skills but are pursuing a degree in business, try listening to music as you study, or create songs lyrics based on the information that you are trying to learn. If you rank high in "spatial intelligence," purchase poster board or "butcher block" paper so that you can map out concepts in a visual manner to facilitate your studies. See additional tips for adapting your study habits to your strengths at http://distancelearn .about.com/od/studyskills/a/studysmart.htm.

> Learning Tip: To work most efficiently, use your identified "intelligences" to shape your study habits.

❖ THE DELIVERY OF INFORMATION

In addition to possessing different types of intelligence, students can vary in the ways that they prefer to receive information. The most common framework for understanding sensory preferences for learning is as follows:

- *Visual* learners most easily comprehend information that they can see, whether in the form of written words or presentations, charts, and figures.

- *Auditory* learners do well at processing information that they hear.

- *Kinesthetic* learners prefer to learn by doing.

- *Tactile* learners prefer "hands on" work "such as building models or doing laboratory experiments."[4]

In face-to-face classes, all students receive a uniform experience in their exposure to information despite their personal learning styles. While instructors might utilize a mix of lecture, PowerPoint presentations, discussions, and assignment of lab work, the logistics of a face-to-face classroom make it so that all students have a common learning experience regardless of their varying sensory preferences. Those who are primarily visual may therefore struggle to a greater extent in classes that are based on lectures or lab work, while those who learn best by doing may have more difficulty in a class that is heavily based on written materials or lecture.

In the online classroom, more instructors are beginning to realize the potential of online learning to account for individual variations by conveying the same information in a variety of formats. They may provide charts as well as podcasts, and discussions as well as supplementary videos. Some programs have students order lab materials for hands-on learning in their home, and others offer internships to provide more immersive learning experiences for their students. Even where instructors have yet to tap into the recent advancements in instructional technology, online students are well situated to adapt their own learning to their preferences and skills. Publishing companies increasingly offer online supplements to their textbooks that include features such as videos, audio files, and self-assessments. There are also online tools—some free, and some available for a reasonable charge—that enable students to convert information into a format more conducive to their learning. Some more specific tips for each sensory preference follow.

Visual learners: If you prefer to receive information visually, you may do well simply reading from your textbook or other course materials, or you may benefit from seeking out diagrams and other types of visual representations. If you are willing to sort through files to find reliable sources, you can search the Internet for PowerPoint presentations and other visual materials that have been posted by instructors at other schools. If you have difficulty finding relevant files, take it upon yourself to map or illustrate the information that your instructor has provided. This might involve simply taking pen to paper; if you prefer to work electronically (rather than on paper), though, try presentation software such as the free download available at www.smartdraw.com to create your study materials.

Auditory learners: You can do an online search for audio files relevant to your topic of study. For example, Apple offers a number of freely accessible podcasts through their iTunes service. (See http://www.apple.com/itunes/podcasts/ for additional guidance.) If you have difficulty finding reliable sources on your topic of study, you can make your own audio files by recording yourself reading your school materials on a small tape recorder, or with an online tool such as Audacity (http://audacity.sourceforge.net/). Auditory learners may also benefit from engaging others in discussion regarding their schoolwork. If you are not in a position to discuss the material with your classmates "by voice," consider talking to your friends or loved ones about what you are studying. Finally, while not all online instructors will be willing to have phone contact with students, some openly distribute their phone number, and others are willing to call students upon request. If you are struggling with some aspect of the material, explore whether your instructor is willing to explain it over the phone.

Kinesthetic learners: If you learn best by "doing," look for opportunities to use interactive software relevant to the topics at hand. When you learn theoretical information, consider how that information might be applied in "real-world" situations. Look for examples within your textbook and other course materials. Finally, if your online school offers internships at local agencies, take advantage of the opportunity.

Tactile learners: As with kinesthetic learners, you may benefit from the use of interactive computer programs. Consider taking frequent breaks as you work and getting up to stretch and walk around. If relevant to your field, try to obtain "hands-on" labs that you can do at home. You might also search YouTube (www.youtube.com) for videos that demonstrate or explain the hands-on processes relevant to your topic of study.

> *Learning Tip: If you can't find materials in the classroom that fit with your sensory learning preference, create your own.*

❖ KOLB'S LEARNING STYLES

In addition to holding variant strengths and sensory preferences, students can differ in the ways that they approach the information that has been presented to them. One of the better-known frameworks for understanding students' different thought processes was proposed by

David Kolb, who identified four learning styles based on where learners fall upon two scales:

- Concrete Experience (feeling)—Abstract Conceptualization (thinking)
- Reflective Observation (watching)—Active Experimentation (doing)[5]

According to this framework, all individuals can learn to some extent through feeling, thinking, watching, *and* doing. Being strong at abstract conceptualization does not preclude your potential to learn through concrete experience, nor vice versa. Still, students tend to have a preference or affinity for one side of each scale. The strength of students' preferences along these two dimensions is what determines their learning style.

Students who prefer to learn through "concrete experiences" focus on the details of specific incidents and their practical implications. By contrast, those who have a proclivity for "abstract conceptualization" place greater emphasis on identifying patterns than on the details of specific experiences, and may be inclined to have an interest in theory rather than practice.[6] According to Kolb, individuals also vary in their emphasis on "watching" relative to "doing." Those who prefer to learn through observation take pleasure in understanding different viewpoints and identifying the meaning and implications of the way that things are. Those who learn by doing emphasize results over reflection.[7]

Based on Kolb's belief that individuals' learning styles are shaped by their combination of preferences on these two scales, he identified four resultant possibilities:

- Accommodator (Doing + Feeling)
- Diverger (Watching + Feeling)
- Converger (Doing + Thinking)
- Assimilator (Watching + Thinking)

Accommodator (Doing + Feeling). Those who emphasize "doing" over "watching" and "feeling" over "thinking" are particularly strong at getting things done, even when there is some risk inherent to taking action. They are quick to adapt when they notice that a particular approach is not effective. This learning style will help you stay regimented in your approach to your schoolwork—learners who fall in this category may be particularly well-equipped to identify and maintain

Figure 6.1	Kolb's Learning Styles	
	Active Experimentation (Doing)	**Reflective Observation (Watching)**
Concrete Experiences (Feeling)	*Accommodators are willing to take risks to get things done, and are quick to adapt when they notice that a particular approach is not effective.*	*Divergers are good at considering a topic from many angles and identifying potential implications.*
Abstract Conceptualization (Thinking)	*Convergers are practical, task-oriented problem-solvers who tend to be good in areas that involve highly technical information.*	*Assimilators are good at thinking of the "big picture" and identifying inconsistencies in information or theoretical models.*

Source: Kolb, 1984.

productive study habits because of their determination to complete tasks. Still, accommodators' focus on doing what it takes to get things done can sometimes make them appear impatient to others.[8] If you are an accommodator and agree that others sometimes perceive you as impatient, you can try to compensate by consciously taking more time to think through the possible benefits of others' approaches and ideas.

Diverger (Watching + Feeling). These individuals emphasize both concrete experiences and reflective observation. Divergent learners work well at considering a topic from many angles and identifying their potential implications. They are also strong at brainstorming, analysis, and integrating different ideas into cohesive, meaningful frameworks. This learning style will support your ability to contribute meaningfully and respectfully on the discussion boards and in other written assignments.

Converger (Doing + Thinking). These individuals are skilled at problem-solving in practical and task-oriented situations. This learning style will support you in courses that involve highly technical information. As an online student, this type of analytic approach will support your ability to grasp complex relationships, be they mathematical, sociological, or otherwise. Convergers may be somewhat less adept at navigating social interactions due to their tendency to focus on the examination of "technical tasks and problems."[9] If you believe that this description fits you, take more time when posting to the discussion boards and sending e-mails to make sure that you have fully considered the perspective of your reader. For example, if you were to respond to a classmate's posting in an Ethics class in which a fellow student has shared a personal ethical struggle from his or her past, instead of jumping into how you would handle such a situation, take a sentence to express sympathy or understanding for your classmate.

Assimilator (Watching + Thinking). This style aligns with the ability to pull ideas together into a meaningful framework, similar to divergers; the distinction, though, is that assimilators are more concerned with abstract ideas than practical implications, and as with convergers the focus is on the material and ideas at hand rather than people. Assimilators will be good at thinking about the "big picture," and identifying inconsistencies in information or theoretical models. This may support your ability to ask targeted questions on the discussion board and to comprehend theoretical concepts within your courses.

❖ OTHER CONSIDERATIONS IN LEARNING STYLE

This chapter only showcased a handful of the many frameworks that have been set forth by psychologists and educational experts for understanding how people learn. You may find additional considerations equally pertinent to the effectiveness of your studies. For example, some people complete their work more easily when they first wake up, whereas others have overwhelming "night owl" tendencies. Some may work well in a highly structured study environment, whereas others prefer to spread their work around them on the floor or curl up on the couch with their laptop (see Chapter 3 for more information on locating a suitable work environment). Some may find that they work best independently, whereas others like to work in groups. If you find yourself struggling with your studies, try doing a search on "learning styles" online. You should be able to find an abundance of frameworks and self-assessments to help you better understand how you learn and sites that provide tips to support your efforts.

❖ CONCLUSION

Every student has strengths that can be utilized in their learning. This chapter provided a few basic frameworks to help you understand the different types of intelligences that you possess, the sensory preferences that you hold, and the ways in which you process information. Use the information that you learned about your own strengths, preferences, and tendencies to guide you in your studies. Also recognize that this information was not an exhaustive account of the factors that may be relevant to learning. You will be best-served if you commit to engagement in ongoing self-reflection regarding what works best for you.

REFLECTION QUESTIONS

1. Describe a recent experience where you had to learn something new. What did you learn, and how difficult was it for you? What can you learn from that experience?

2. Of the "multiple intelligences" listed in this chapter, which do you think represents *your* greatest strength? Explain your thoughts.

3. Do you prefer to learn through visual, auditory, kinesthetic, or tactile sensory inputs? How might you adapt your studies to fit with your preferences?

4. Do you see connections between your learning strengths and your selected field of study? If so, explain how it can benefit you. If not, explain how your strengths might still be beneficial in your chosen field.

CHAPTER CHECKLIST

☐ Locate and take a "multiple intelligences" assessment.

☐ Locate and take a "learning styles inventory."

☐ Brainstorm at least five ideas regarding how you can adjust your study habits to better fit with your learning style and preferences.

RELATED RESOURCES

Auditory Learning Aids	http://www.apple.com/itunes/podcasts/
Auditory Learning Aids	http://audacity.sourceforge.net/
Study Tips	http://distancelearn.about.com/od/studyskills/a/studysmart.htm
Visual/Auditory Learning Aids	www.youtube.com
Visual Learning Aids	www.smartdraw.com

❖ NOTES

1. Gardner, H. (2006). *Multiple Intelligences: New Horizons.* New York: Basic Books.

2. See page 9 of Gardner, 2006.

3. See pages 14–15 of Gardner, 2006.

4. See page 89 of Reid, J. (1987). The learning style preferences of ESL students. *TESOL Quarterly, 21*(1), 87–111.

5. See Kolb, D. (1984). *Experiential Learning: Experience as the Source of Learning and Development.* Englewood Cliffs, NJ: Prentice-Hall, Inc.

6. See pages 68–69 of Kolb, 1984.

7. See pages 68–69 of Kolb, 1984.

8. See page 78 of Kolb, 1984.

9. See page 77 of Kolb, 1984.

7

Written Communication

❖ INTRODUCTION

College students, online or otherwise, are likely to spend countless hours each semester tending to research papers and other written assignments. What is unique about online courses is the extent to which students rely on the written word for school-related communications. While some online courses contain embedded audio or video components, much of the interaction that takes place is text-based. This chapter seeks to support readers in the development of effective communication skills within this unique social context.

❖ COMPUTER-MEDIATED COMMUNICATION, ACADEMIC STYLE

In traditional classrooms, communication tends to take place in widely recognized and commonly understood forms. A student raises his hand, and the instructor knows to call on him. The instructor casts a disapproving glance to a student who is whispering to a classmate, and she knows to return her attention to the lecture in progress. If a student makes a statement that inadvertently offends others, he may be able to quickly detect the error of his ways based on facial expressions, leading to an apology or clarification; if not, the instructor is typically present to diffuse the tension.

Navigating an online classroom is a bit different. Unlike a face-to-face environment, students must learn to interact without the benefit of cues such as tone, body language, or facial expressions. Since the written word doesn't inherently reflect the grimace, smile, or mischievous twinkle in the eye of the "speaker," other conventions must be relied upon to convey tone. In addition, since many interactions are asynchronous in nature, the instructor may not be online when potentially problematic exchanges occur, placing a greater responsibility with students to prevent potential misunderstandings and, when misunderstandings do occur, to respond in a manner that prevents further escalation of the situation.

Students may face a number of questions as they first adjust to communicating in this unique environment. Those who are new to online interactions may be unfamiliar with the conventions that are commonly used to convey tone. Even students who have posted to public discussion boards on anything from a personal health condition to the latest plot twist on their favorite television show may feel uncertainty regarding the expectations in an academic environment. This chapter supports students of all backgrounds as they learn conventions for different types of school-related communications—discussion board postings, e-mails, and formal writing assignments.

❖ DISCUSSION BOARDS

The heart and soul of many online classrooms is the discussion board; hybrid classes will sometimes contain an online component solely to make use of this tool. The discussion board provides an outstanding opportunity to engage in critical exchanges about the course material and to flesh out relevant ideas and questions regarding topics set forth by the instructor. Many students enjoy this area of the classroom. In many cases, they are able to share personal experiences that relate to the discussion at hand, an opportunity that facilitates a sense of community[1] and allows students to benefit from each other's oft-diverse life experiences. Since this also tends to be a graded component of the class, a few guidelines will facilitate your success:

- Follow directions
- Stay on-topic

- Be part of the solution

- Read everything before posting

- Take a tempered approach to the contributions of others

- Follow the rules of online etiquette

- Limit your text-talk

- Use spell check

- Stay honest

Follow Directions

Some instructors may specifically ask students to make discussion board postings based on personal opinion or experiences, while others will expect contributions to be based on research. Instructors may also set specific expectations regarding how frequently you should post, the number of postings required for each discussion, and the length of those postings. Look for these types of expectations in the syllabus, announcements area, e-mails, or within the discussion board itself, and then strive to meet them—these are the benchmarks on which you will be graded. Instructors often have established deadlines for each discussion; pay attention to those dates, as you may be unable to earn credit after they have passed.

While "following directions" may seem intuitive, you may at some point find yourself faced with a discussion board topic regarding which you are particularly passionate, increasing the temptation to type out a response based solely on personal opinion, or you may find yourself struggling to organize your time in a manner that allows you to meet your instructor's expectations for level of involvement. If you find yourself receiving low grades on discussion board involvement, don't get discouraged—reflect on which expectations you have struggled to meet, and strive to address those shortcomings moving forward. It may take a week or two to learn to tailor your contributions to the expectations of your instructor, or to adjust your schedule to accommodate an acceptable level of involvement. A learning curve is to be expected; if you work through this adjustment period and heed the directions and feedback provided by your instructor, you will soon find yourself making model postings and receiving grades that reflect your dedication.

> *Learning Tip: Take some time at the beginning of each term to become familiar with each instructor's expectations.*

Stay On-Topic

Discussion boards are intended to facilitate interaction on course-related topics. Unfortunately, they are also rife with the temptation to get off-track. Students who are excited to see postings from others that they have come to know during the semester may wrongfully succumb to the temptation to catch up on personal matters on the discussion board. In working to resist this temptation, it may help to envision how such off-topic contributions would play out in a traditional classroom; just as a student wouldn't jump up in the middle of a classroom discussion on Eastern philosophical thought and shout, "Hey, Bernice—how are the kids? Good to see you again!" communication on the board should stick to the topic at hand.

There is no such thing as "whispering to the person next to you" on the discussion board. While developing friendships with fellow online students can provide a much-needed support system when things get tough, it is simply important to make sure that personal communications are channeled through appropriate outlets. If you have a personal question or a story to tell one of your fellow classmates, turn to e-mail or instant messaging; some classrooms will even have a separate area set up specifically to provide students with a "virtual space" to socialize. (See Chapter 4 for additional outlets for personal communication available to support the building of friendships with classmates who are separated by geographic distance.)

While the "how are the kids" example provided above was quite blatant, discussions sometimes get sidetracked through more subtle mechanisms. Reading about one topic may spur thoughts on another, which then branches out to another, and so forth. A student may read a question about the death penalty that reminds him of something that he read regarding the nation's prison system, which may bring to mind criminal trials, which may prompt the memory of a recent episode of *Law & Order: SVU*. Following the natural flow of thought on the discussion boards can lead further and further away from the original topic. Soon, students may find themselves participating in a discussion that bears little, if any, relationship to the topic at hand, and the instructor is likely to grade accordingly.

There is an easy way to prevent this kind of pattern: Before posting a contribution, double-check to make sure that what you have written relates directly to the topic or question that had been posted by the instructor. There is nothing wrong with drawing on personal examples in a posting if your instructor supports doing so, but any incorporation of such material should relate directly back to the topic at hand. This self-check will prevent you from contributing to the discussion getting off-track.

Be Part of the Solution

If you see others start to get off topic on the discussion board, it does not provide license to follow suit. In fact, students who get side-tracked are likely to see a reduction in their discussion board grades as a result. If you find yourself becoming distracted by the postings of others, a more productive response is to take steps to help steer the discussion back on course. You have as much power to shape the discussions as your fellow students.

How can you help in a situation in which you witness your fellow students getting side-tracked? One option is to simply stay focused on the topic at hand; the more students that focus on the work to be done, the less the discussion will get off-track. A second option is to make a friendly posting directing your classmates to more appropriate channels: "Susan, I'm so glad to hear that the kids are doing well! Let's get caught up by instant messenger sometime, so that we don't pull this thread off-topic." If you are troubled by others' postings but uncomfortable addressing the situation yourself, the third option is to simply e-mail your instructor to alert him or her to any issues on the board. Instructors may have a number of tools at their disposal to address the offending post(s): they may choose to remove the posting, address the student offline, or, if necessary, address the class as a whole. Regardless of which of these options you choose, don't approach the student in a confrontational manner within the discussion, as doing so risks aggravating the situation and distracting the class even further.

Reread Everything Before Posting

When typing a discussion board response, students may sometimes become so focused on making a particular point that they fail to realize how their posting will be interpreted by others. It is easy to come across more harshly than intended; reading over your contribution before posting enables you to catch and correct nuances that you may not have intended when writing. If you are unsure of whether your contribution might be misinterpreted, consider approaching a friend or relative for a second opinion.

Take a Tempered Approach to the Contributions of Others

Even with all parties putting forth their best effort to avoid potential misunderstandings, no student is immune. If you are upset by a classmate's posting, it may be useful to walk away from the computer for a few minutes, and then reread the contribution with an open mind to see whether you may have misread what he or she had intended. If the posting still seems inappropriate in some way, you might choose to simply disregard it, or to tactfully request that the student clarify, or to approach the instructor for guidance on how to handle the situation. Little is to be gained from approaching a fellow student (or your instructor, for that matter!) in a confrontational tone.

> *Learning Tip: Don't engage in confrontations on the board. If you feel that someone has posted something offensive, notify your instructor immediately.*

Follow the Rules of Online Etiquette

There are some simple steps that can be taken to lessen the likelihood of misunderstandings or conflict on the discussion board. First, avoid the use of all capital letters—in online communications, typing in all CAPS is considered "yelling," and shouting has no place in an academic environment! Second, when you disagree with classmates, avoid making comments that might be construed as personal attacks; all of your postings should be focused on the discussion at hand, not on the personal qualities or beliefs of others. Finally, use emoticons (icons indicating emotion) to your advantage—while overuse of emoticons is likely to come across as unprofessional, a strategically placed smiling face (created by typing a colon and an end-parenthesis) can help to communicate a friendly or joking tone to those reading your contributions.

Limit Your Text-Talk (LYTT)

We live in a world of fast-paced communications; "texting" in particular—sending text messages from one's cell phone—has become incredibly commonplace in recent years. Since texting on a standard cell phone entails hitting a key as many as three times to type just one letter, the desire for efficiency has contributed to the widespread use of abbreviations to communicate common phrases. "Thank you" becomes "ty," "laughing out loud" becomes "lol," and a response of approval or satisfaction becomes, simply, :). The complexities of texting have also contributed to users dropping the use of punctuation and capitalization. Acronyms, abbreviations, and emoticons have now worked their way into other communication contexts, such as informal online chats. While these are useful adaptations in some social contexts, most "text talk" should be left at the proverbial classroom door.

There are at least two benefits to minimizing, or entirely avoiding the use of, "text talk" in online courses. First, typing words in their entirety facilitates communication among all members of the classroom, including those who have not acclimated to the "texting" culture and may therefore struggle with deciphering the potentially complex codes typed by their classmates. Second, for those who are quite skilled at "text-talk," relying on formal writing within the classroom—including the conventional use of punctuation and capital letters—assists in preparing for other social situations that warrant formal communication, such as most workplace environments. Some people, including many employers and professors, do still expect you to capitalize at the beginning of a sentence, use punctuation, and actually type out words in their entirety. :)

While generally speaking you should err on the side of formal communications in the classroom, as with many rules, there are some exceptions. Due to the potential for misunderstandings, some instructors will be accepting, or even encouraging, of some of the most basic symbols and abbreviations to indicate the tone of your communications on the discussion board or in synchronous chats. The smiling face is the most commonly invoked emoticon, and an occasional "lol" may be warranted to indicate to fellow students that you understood the lighthearted nature of one of their comments. Watch your instructor's communications for cues—does he or she throw in an occasional smiley face?—and, if in doubt, ask your instructor how they feel about the use of these conventions before you utilize them in the classroom.

Use Spell Check

Even the most adept writer is not immune to errors. Some students have a long history of difficulty with spelling, and even the best spellers may mistype as a result of typing too quickly. While an occasional misspelled word is part of being human, those reading your contributions can be distracted by errors. Reread your work prior to posting so that you can identify and correct typos, and make full use of any other tools available to assist with further refinement of your work. If your discussion platform has a "spell check" option, use it. If not, it may be helpful to first type your contributions into a word processing program that does have a spell check feature, such as Microsoft Word or WordPerfect, and then copy-and-paste your work after you have made any necessary corrections.

Learning Tip: Always scan your contributions before posting to confirm relevancy and to give yourself a chance to catch and correct any errors or misstatements.

Attend Class When You Are at Your Best (Relatively Speaking)

One of the best features of online education is the ability to complete your schoolwork almost anywhere, anytime. One of the potential issues with online education is also the ability to complete your schoolwork almost anywhere, anytime! The convenience, coupled with the sense of anonymity that comes with the online environment, may make some students lax in their judgment regarding when and in what condition they "show up for class." Your life circumstances may necessitate that you post to the discussion board when tired, but you may at other times find yourself tempted to log into your classroom while dazed with the flu, groggy with pain medication, or otherwise incapacitated.

While sometimes an impending deadline may render immediate participation necessary, the potential for miscommunication on the boards makes it beneficial to type with as clear of a head as your life situation allows. If you are concerned about your judgment because you are having difficulty thinking due to illness or other factors, consider asking a friend or family member to review your postings prior to submission to get an outside perspective on whether changes may be needed. If you have extenuating circumstances that temporarily interfere with your concentration, such as a high fever or a short-term prescription for pain medication, it may be worthwhile to reach out to your instructor to inquire about the possibility of a brief extension. You will likely be able to complete your work more efficiently once the temporary condition has passed, and typing with a "clear head" will minimize the likelihood of contributions that may be misconstrued by others.

Stay Honest

As with any schoolwork, any wording or ideas that are not your own should be properly cited on the discussion board (see Chapter 9 for more guidance on citing sources). If you find relevant information on the Internet that you would like to share with classmates, as best practice post the link rather than drawing extensive quotes from the Web site. If you run into a difficult circumstance, it isn't worth cutting and pasting information from elsewhere in an effort to meet the minimum expectations for participation; instructors have seen it all, and they are not likely to take kindly to contributions that are not your original work. If you find yourself thinking that your only option is to cut corners, it should be your cue to approach your instructor to explore the possibility of an extension, or to reevaluate the manner in which you have organized your time (see Chapter 3 for assistance with time management).

❖ E-MAILS

E-mail has become a popular tool for asynchronous communication in recent years and is commonly used in online learning environments. "E-mail" refers to a mechanism for sending electronic messages (e-mails) from one personalized account to another. As stated in Chapter 2, many schools will provide each student with an e-mail account to facilitate communication with instructors and fellow students. While some instructors may provide students with their phone numbers, in most cases e-mail will be the primary mechanism for one-on-one communication.

E-mail allows students to communicate information that they would prefer not to share in a more public forum, such as requests for extensions due to personal circumstances. E-mail can also be used to ask instructors questions about the course content or the expectations for a given assignment. Since e-mails are usually not graded, students may be somewhat less formal in these communications; still, a few conventions should be followed:

Polish. In e-mails as with any online communication, follow the basic rules of etiquette—do not use all capital letters, and be sure to invoke the use of a smiling face emoticon if you are concerned that a light-hearted portion of your message may be misinterpreted. Take the time to use spell-check out of respect for the recipient of your message. Abide by standard conventions for writing, such as the use of capitalization and punctuation. Finally, take the time to reread your e-mail before sending, as this may allow you to catch and correct any phrasing that may be lacking in clarity.

Professionalism. Even though e-mails are relatively private in nature, they should still be drafted in a manner commensurate with a professional environment. Share only those personal details that are directly relevant, such as your reason for requesting an extension. Refrain from sending e-mails that are not related to your coursework, such as jokes that you have received from friends.

Finally, when using your school-provided e-mail account, keep in mind that your school may have policies regulating its use of technology, and may reserve the right to monitor your account; draft your messages accordingly, and use a separate e-mail account for any non-school-related communications.

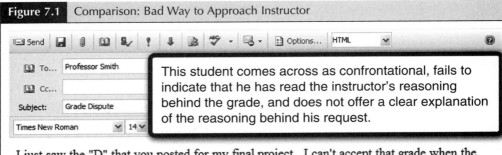

Figure 7.1   Comparison: Bad Way to Approach Instructor

This student comes across as confrontational, fails to indicate that he has read the instructor's reasoning behind the grade, and does not offer a clear explanation of the reasoning behind his request.

I just saw the "D" that you posted for my final project. I can't accept that grade when the paper was only late because of a technical error that wasn't my fault. I worked very hard on that paper, and deserve much higher. This pulls down my GPA, and I'm usually an "A" student! Please alleviate this issue so that I don't have to pursue this with the Dean.

Johnny

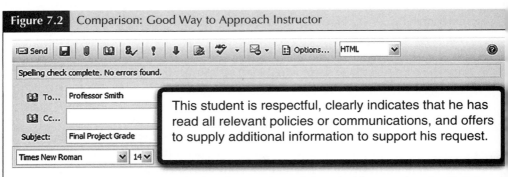

Figure 7.2   Comparison: Good Way to Approach Instructor

This student is respectful, clearly indicates that he has read all relevant policies or communications, and offers to supply additional information to support his request.

I just checked my grade on the final project, and noted that I had been assigned a "D." I read your comments, and understand your concern about the paper being submitted three days late. Unfortunately, I had been unable to request an extension because my computer had completely crashed.

I am writing to request that you reconsider my grade based on this information. I would be happy to provide verification of my issue from the technician who worked on my computer.

I apologize for not approaching you on this matter earlier, and thank you in advance for your consideration,

Johnny

❖ FORMAL WRITING ASSIGNMENTS

Online courses often entail projects, essay exams, or other types of formal written assignments. Many of the skills developed for discussion board and e-mail communications will apply to paper-writing—if you follow directions carefully, cite your sources, stay on-topic, avoid text-talk, use spell-check, and reread for errors prior to submission, you are likely to do well! Still, there a couple of specifics that distinguish the demands of paper-writing from other forms of written communication:

> *Organization.* Written assignments will typically be longer than standard e-mails or discussion board postings, and may necessitate a more complex interweaving of ideas and information. This elevates the importance of maintaining strong organization within your work. Different types of assignments will have different organizational conventions, so pay close attention to the guidance provided by your instructor. Many schools have resources to assist students in writing papers, ranging from recommendations for writing-focused texts, to writing centers that provide tutors or paper review services (see Chapter 4 for some possible resources). Make full use of the sources that are available to you.

> *Increased Formality.* While all school-related communications necessitate some level of professionalism, smiling faces and other non-traditional writing conventions are often accepted (in moderation) in discussions and e-mails to help prevent misunderstandings. By contrast, instructors expect that students will invest enough time in research papers, essay exams, and other standard writing assignments to be able to clearly communicate ideas without relying on these tools. Bear this in mind as you draft your assignments.

❖ CONCLUSION

This chapter outlined some of the peculiarities inherent to communication in an online academic environment, and provided guidance for writing on the discussion boards, in e-mails, and in formal assignments. Chapter 4 identified some resources to support you, and Chapters 8 and 9 will provide additional information to assist with research-based writing. If you have lingering questions about what is expected of you, reach out to your instructors for clarification; they are there to help. Finally, if you have any concerns about your writing skills, embrace online learning as a great opportunity (and incentive) to improve your skills. Nobody is born a good writer; learning to write well is a process for even the best authors. Explore the resources that are available to you, and learn from the feedback provided by your instructor.

REFLECTION QUESTIONS

1. Do you consider yourself a strong writer? If not, what can you do to strengthen your writing skills?

2. Do you think that there is a greater likelihood that miscommunication will occur in a face-to-face environment or online? Explain your answer.

CHAPTER CHECKLIST

☐ Locate your instructor's expectations for discussion board participation.

☐ If you don't have a personal e-mail account, establish one so that you are not tempted to use your school account for personal communications.

☐ Identify resources that can assist you as you further develop your writing skills. If your school has a writing center, find out how to access it.

RELATED RESOURCES

Dictionary	www.dictionary.com
E-mail Etiquette	www.emailreplies.com
Emoticon Guide	www.pcworld.com/article/88686/lol_a_guide_to_ internet_lingo_and_emoticons.html
Online Learning Etiquette	http://online.uwc.edu/technology/onlEtiquette.asp
Online Learning Etiquette	www.netmanners.com
Thesaurus	www.thesaurus.com

❖ NOTE

1. See O'Neal, K. (2009). The comparison between asynchronous online discussion and traditional classroom discussion in an undergraduate education course. *MERLOT Journal of Online Learning and Teaching, 5*(1), 88–96.

8

Conducting Quality
Research for Your
Online Class

❖ INTRODUCTION

Many college courses will require that students conduct some form
of research project, or that they otherwise support their written
work (such as discussion board postings) with information found
from other sources. It can be time-consuming to find quality information on a topic, which can lead to frustration among students.
Still, learning to conduct research is an integral part of receiving a
quality education. Conducting research provides more in-depth
exposure to relevant information than what might be provided by
texts or other classroom materials, and it helps students develop
skills that will serve them throughout their careers. This chapter
explains the importance of research and how to assess the reliability
of various sources, and provides guidance for locating sources as an
online student.

❖ WHY RESEARCH?

Research is a central component to many classrooms, online and face-to-face. Some students may chafe at this; it can be time-consuming to locate a number of sources on any given topic and to smoothly integrate information from various sources into a paper. Those who hold strong opinions about emotionally charged topics such as stem-cell research or the death penalty may dislike the idea of having to locate reports on those topics that may not support their perspective. Others may feel that the practice is a waste of time in an age when information seems so readily available through sources such as Wikipedia. Still, learning to conduct quality research in your chosen field may be nearly as important as the specialized knowledge that you will learn in your courses.

Importance of Research

You have likely enrolled in your classes to learn more about a field of personal or professional interest, whether it be biochemistry or nursing, mathematics or psychology. You rely upon instructors and textbooks for up-to-date, relevant, and accurate information in that area. Still, no amount of instruction will provide an exhaustive understanding of a given field; there is always more to be learned. Reading outside materials is one way of expanding learning beyond the confines of the classroom.

Learning to conduct research—to locate your own sources of information about a given topic—will also support you in staying current in your field once you have completed your degree. All fields of study are constantly changing; even something as seemingly static as "history" is revised as new discoveries are made and as time progresses. While course materials often provide students with the most up-to-date information available at that point in time, learning how to locate reliable sources in your field will empower you to access new information as the field continues to develop.

> *Learning Tip: Spend some time learning to conduct quality research, as it is a skill that will prove useful throughout your career.*

Research vs. Opinion

If you already have a strong opinion on your research topic, you may be tempted to selectively pay attention to sources that align with your personal beliefs. To address this tendency, it may be helpful to understand the relationship between research and personal opinions. In part, a college degree reflects your demonstrated ability to set aside personal beliefs and think critically to assess in an educated manner the best factual information available on a given topic. Still, while it is important to be able to identify and critically evaluate reliable information, it may help to know that *academic* conclusions need not shape *personal* beliefs.

Personal beliefs are rarely based entirely upon factual information; your convictions are likely guided by political leanings, upbringing, religious beliefs, and personal experiences. It is entirely valid for you to write a paper concluding that the best available research on the death penalty demonstrates that it does not reduce crime rates, while still holding on to a personal belief that the penalty should be allowable for retributive purposes. Similarly, if the data indicate that the death penalty provides victims with an increased sense of justice, it would be entirely valid to continue to hold on to a personal belief that the death penalty should not be allowed due to religious convictions. Exposing yourself to the best available evidence on all sides of an issue builds your expertise on that issue—it need not entail a change to your personal opinions.

❖ TYPES OF RESOURCES

Quality research begins with locating quality information. It is not hard to find information; we are inundated with it in all aspects of our lives. We hear parents, children, and friends share stories around the dinner table. We watch television and listen to the radio. We see newspaper headlines and peruse the Internet. The ease of access to information in the present day may lead students to feel confident that they are knowledgeable and informed on various topics, but amid Twitter updates, blogs, and major media outlets, not all information is equal. The real trick is learning to assess the extent to which various sources are reliable. This section identifies different categories of sources and explores the strengths and drawbacks of each:

- Personal experiences
- Traditional mass media
- Web sites
- Books
- Academic journals

Personal Experiences

In some cases, you may find that you have had personal experiences that are relevant to your research topic, and may be tempted to include a description of those experiences in your schoolwork. In many ways, those who have personally encountered cancer, divorce, criminal victimization, or other such critical events are indeed "experts," holding a unique and valuable perspective that can only come from experience. In some types of assignments, such as papers that are intended to be persuasive or autobiographical in nature, it may be entirely valid to draw on these personal insights.

Still, while fully valid in their own right, personal experiences may not be appropriate for inclusion in research papers. Assignments that require research are typically intended to develop students' understanding of the broader magnitude and nature of a given phenomenon. When evaluating a personal situation, it is not readily apparent to what extent your experience had been "typical"—representative of common experiences—necessitating that you turn to other sources to gather information.

As one example of the importance of conducting research, consider how the pharmaceutical industry would be different if it relied entirely upon the experiences of just one person. The television ad for a particular drug might simply state, "Take MagicPill X; Jimmy took it, and he hasn't had another heart attack since!" For Jimmy and his family, the apparent success of the pill is an incredibly important matter. For the general public, though, there are many questions that remain unanswered: How common are side effects with this medication? Have others also taken the pill with success, or did Jimmy just get lucky in not having another heart attack? Because we can't know how typical Jimmy's experience is, it is best to not rely upon his personal story in assessing the value of "MagicPill X."

A better understanding of the effects of this pill can be gained by examining the experiences of a larger number of people. In medical trials, how many people taking "MagicPill X" suffered heart attacks, and how did they compare to those who do not take the pill? Does the effectiveness of the pill vary based on characteristics such as the person's age or gender? In most cases, as a college student, you are not likely to be able to access a large number of people to ask them about their experiences with your topic of research directly; luckily, there have likely been scholars and researchers who have already done some legwork on your topic. In the case of "MagicPill X," looking up research studies that have already been conducted would allow you to better assess the potential risks and benefits of the pill and draw educated conclusions regarding its usefulness. The development of this ability to think beyond personal experiences, locate reliable sources, and interpret their meaning is an integral part of college learning, regardless of whether you are studying medicine or business (or any other topic).

> *Learning Tip: While personal experiences are important, they may not be appropriate to include in your school assignments; when in doubt, check with your instructor first.*

Traditional Mass Media

Before the tremendous growth in the use of the Internet, most news was transmitted via television, radio, magazines, or newspapers; since other Web sites will be discussed separately, these sources and their companion Web sites are being referred to collectively as "traditional mass media." These sources are invaluable when students are asked to report on, or analyze media coverage of, current events. In addition, the information contained in these sources is typically accurate; journalists/ reporters often fact-check and tend to depend upon reliable sources for the information that they disseminate.

Despite the general factual accuracy of traditional mass media, there are reasons for hesitation in using these sources in a research paper unless the assignment specifically calls for it. First, decision-makers in media agencies selectively present information in order to increase their viewership/readership. For example, the economy may be more likely to get coverage when it is declining, and crime or disease when they are increasing. News outlets may specifically exclude numbers that are less dramatic, or present statistics in a manner that makes problems seem more severe than they are.

In addition to selectivity, there is the possibility that inaccurate or blatantly biased information could be presented in traditional mass media. Bias is perhaps the most common because as news outlets have proliferated, they have begun to tailor to more specialized markets. Errors can also find their way to the public as news agencies operate under tight deadlines. Rare, but also possible, are cases of reporter fraud.

Due to the many potential drawbacks of relying upon traditional mass media in a research paper, it is recommended that you check with your instructor before referencing such sources. In some cases, instructors may be willing to accept them if other, more reliable sources are also referenced. If you are not allowed to utilize traditional mass media sources for your assignment but you happen to see a news story that contains information that may be helpful to your paper, check to see if the news story makes reference to its source. In some cases, the news will simply be reporting on information published in a book or government report, or provided by a certain agency or expert; if so, then you may be able to locate and utilize the original source within your paper.

Web Sites

In this age of technology, it is common to use the Internet as a resource for information ranging from recipes to current events, celebrity gossip to the most recent sports scores. Upon receiving a research assignment, the first instinct of many computer-savvy students will be to visit Google, enter search terms relevant to their research, and then rely upon the first few sites that appear in the writing of their paper. Unfortunately, this is a matter on which students and instructors rarely see eye-to-eye. While the Internet can be used to access a wealth of reliable sources, ranging from the books of Google Books to the journal articles accessible through many library Web sites or Google Scholar, there is also a good deal of misinformation on the Internet.

Students need to be extremely cautious regarding what they accept as "truth" on the Internet. It can sometimes be difficult to distinguish fact from fiction, as biased parties will sometimes intentionally masquerade as more reliable sources. While doing a study of immigration, the author of this book was once surprised by the information that she found on what appeared to be an official government Web site, only to look more closely and realize that the site was actually hosted by an anti-immigration group. In another case, she searched YouTube to locate an anti-drug public service announcement (PSA) featuring former first lady Nancy Reagan for a sociology class. Luckily she realized before showing the video to the class that it had been altered to make it appear that Mrs. Reagan was advocating drug use.

For those who rely on Internet research for convenience, or those who are unable to readily access hard-copy resources due to other physical constraints, there are some strategies that can be used to delineate "reliable" from "unreliable" Web sites. First, where possible, the sites relied upon should end in ".gov," which indicates an official government Web site. These sites often provide the general public with the ability to download government publications at little or no cost. Government sites are preferred for a couple of reasons. First, government sources tend to have a low level of bias; since government agencies are responsible for regulating many aspects of society, they have compelling reason to rely upon the most robust information available in those areas, ranging from education to health to national defense.

The government also has more access to funding and resources than other types of agencies, resulting in impressive research capabilities. The best example of this is the U.S. Census. Every 10 years, the Census Bureau engages in a massive effort to collect information on every individual living in the United States. If a standard university researcher would want to employ a survey of similar magnitude, assuming 300 million residents and a cost of 44 cents per stamp, it would cost $132,000,000 for stamps alone, not counting the expenses of paper, printing, envelopes, and staff to process the surveys! Most researchers, or research agencies, do not come close to matching the government's resources or research capabilities.

The Web sites of educational institutions are delineated with an ".edu" and are also generally thought to be reliable and appropriate sources for school papers. College or university professors are often considered the experts in their field, and they may post their research to their school's Web site. Still, .edu sites sometimes include personal or political views, so it is not a "given" that they will be acceptable sources.

Check with your professor regarding whether sites that end in .org are acceptable resources. This marker generally distinguishes sites that belong to nonprofit organizations. While some of these agencies, such as the American Heart Association, are respected for producing reliable data, others may be more substantially biased. A paper written based on information found at www.prolife.org is likely to be dramatically different than one based on www.prochoice.org. While the organizations that run each site are likely respected within certain circles for their cause work, the information contained on each site will also predictably reflect the views of the hosts of the site, rendering them both a poor choice for most college papers.

Many students are tempted to rely upon the online encyclopedia found at www.wikipedia.org as a starting point in research. While it is now broadly accepted that Wikipedia contains errors at only a slightly higher rate than traditional encyclopedias,[1] most college instructors expect students to rely on more comprehensive sources. This site—or any type of encyclopedia, online or in hard copy—may be a good starting point if you need clarification on a particular concept before locating more reliable sources, but it is likely a poor choice as one of your cited resources.

Learning Tip: When using Internet sources, stick to .gov or .edu Web sites unless your instructor specifically asks for or approves otherwise.

Most remaining Internet sites will be either ".com" or ".net" sites; both of these usually indicate that sites are hosted to private individuals or industries. These are typically not desirable sources when it comes to academic research unless you are specifically studying what people or businesses post on these sites. For example, a marketing instructor may ask students to examine the use of logos on certain retail Web sites and then report on what they found.

Books

Nonfiction books are often great sources of information, as they are typically subject to review for accuracy before making it to the bookshelves. Particularly respectable are books that are published by university presses, which have a high standard for content and often contain the results of research studies or the work of prominent theorists. By contrast, books that are targeted for a popular audience— those published by non-university presses—may leave out details that would be pertinent in assessing the reliability of the information that they contain, and therefore should be used with some caution.

Since most popular chain bookstores stock their shelves with books intended for the general public, their selection of solid academic resources may be limited. A good starting point for locating scholarly books, then, would be your school's library if you are near a campus, or a nearby public library. Many libraries now host Web sites that enable you to search their inventory for books from the convenience of your own home, and to request interlibrary loans from affiliated libraries.

While in most cases you will still need to travel to a library to pick up any books that you find, online schools with a geographically disperse student body may offer to-your-door mail service for their collection. Some books are now also accessible online in electronic format, in whole or in part, most notably through a feature of Google called Google Books. (Simply visit books.google.com in your Web browser and enter search terms relevant to your research topic.) For those interested in building a personal collection of books in their area of interest, most popular bookstores maintain merchant Web sites that allow access to a broader selection of books than is available at their brick-and-mortar stores. A number of general online merchant sites, such as www.amazon.com and www.ebay.com, also offer inventories of books available for order.

Academic Journals

Academic journals are periodicals that are published by academically oriented organizations (often universities). Journals provide scholars with an outlet for research findings or theoretical developments that are significant in their fields of study, but which may not be enticing enough to draw a broad general audience. Scholars often read academic journals in their field to stay abreast of current research. Many of these publications employ a rigorous screening and editorial process known as "peer review" for the papers that ultimately end up between their pages; in this process, experts in the relevant field of study evaluate the papers based on accuracy and the quality of the research methods employed. This process renders academic journals the most consistently reliable source of information for students looking to gain a deeper understanding of their topic of study.

> *Learning Tip: Academic journals often contain the most respected information available in a given field.*

❖ RESEARCHING FOR YOUR ONLINE CLASS

As you work to juggle schooling with other obligations, and as you settle into a routine that involves completing most schoolwork in front of a computer screen and on your own schedule, you may be happy to learn that you can access most types of resources—not just Web sites—online:

- *Traditional Mass Media.* In order to maintain their viability in the present landscape, traditional mass media outlets have begun to maintain a corollary presence online.[2] Many newscasts and articles are now available for online access. If you see a news story that you would like to locate online, try utilizing an Internet search engine such as Google to find it, or one of the following aggregate Web sites:
  - Television station Web sites: www.high-techproductions.com/u_s.htm
  - Newspaper Web sites: www.usnpl.com. The Web site for your school's library may also offer a searchable database of newspaper and/or magazine archives.
- *Books.* In some cases, you may need to physically travel to a local library or bookstore to obtain the book(s) that you need. Still, some books can be accessed online in a number of ways:
  - New books can be purchased from retailers at sites such as www.borders.com and www.barnesandnoble.com.

Figure 8.1 Search Interface From a Library Web Site

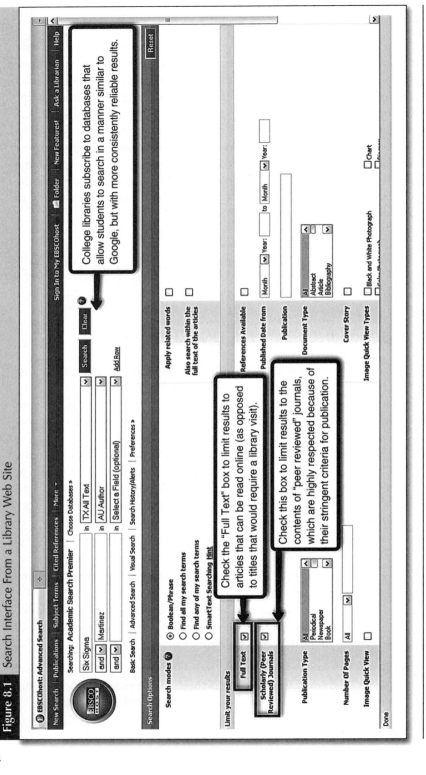

Source: EBSCO Publishing.

- o Used books can be ordered through resellers at sites such as www.ebay.com and www.amazon.com.
- o Sometimes referred to as an "electronic book" or "e-book" option, some books are available online in their entirety through your school or public library Web site, or general sites such as www.books.google.com. Your textbooks may also be available in an electronic version through the publisher.
- o Some books can be downloaded in electronic format for portable viewing devices such as the Kindle (www.kindle.com) or Sony Reader (www.ebookstore.sony.com/reader).

- *Academic Journals.* Your school pays to allow students to access journal articles through its library and likely provides electronic access to them through the library's Web site. You may also be able to find academic journal articles online through public search engines such as Google Scholar (www.scholar.google.com), but access to the full text of these articles may require payment—so your best bet is to work through your school's library.

❖ CONCLUSION

With so much information "at our fingertips," it can seem daunting to try to distinguish fact from fiction or bias. The good news is that it is possible to have a fair amount of confidence in the information found in books, journal articles, and .gov sites in particular, and many of these sources are now accessible via the Internet. Since individual instructors may be more strict or lenient than what is outlined here, it is important to always refer to course materials or consult with your instructor regarding the types of resources that are allowable for a given course.

REFLECTION QUESTIONS

1. Why is it important to conduct research?
2. What are some signs that indicate the reliability of a source?

CHAPTER CHECKLIST

☐ Find out whether your school's library offers electronic access to journals; if so, take notes on how to access them.

☐ Locate and bookmark the Web sites for three local traditional news outlets.

☐ Identify three reliable sources relevant to your field.

RELATED RESOURCES

Books	http://books.google.com
Books—For Purchase	www.half.com
Books—For Purchase	www.amazon.com/books
Books—For Purchase	www.barnesandnoble.com
Books—For Purchase	www.borders.com
Web site	www.wikipedia.com
Scholarly Articles	http://scholar.google.com
Books—For Purchase (Kindle)	www.kindle.com
Books—For Purchase (Sony Reader)	www.ebookstore.sony.com/reader
Traditional Mass Media	www.cnn.com
Traditional Mass Media	www.abcnews.com
Traditional Mass Media	www.foxnews.com
Traditional Mass Media—Links to TV Web sites	www.high-techproductions.com/u_s.htm
Traditional Mass Media—Links to Newspaper Web sites	www.usnpl.com

❖ NOTES

1. Giles, J. (2005). Special report: Internet encyclopedias go head to head. *Nature, 438*(15), 900–901.

2. Alterman, E. (2008). The death and life of the American newspaper. *The New Yorker.* Accessed from http://www.newyorker.com/reporting/2008/03/31/080331fa_fact_alterman

9

Citing Your Sources

❖ INTRODUCTION

Unless you are taking one of the few online courses based entirely upon quizzes and multiple choice tests, you are likely to write—a lot—as part of your coursework. From discussion board contributions to formal papers, much of this writing is likely to be based on what you have read in textbooks or other sources. Whenever you draw from the work of others, you are expected to give credit accordingly. With the understanding that many online students may be new to academic writing, or may have struggled with properly citing sources in the past, this chapter provides step-by-step support to students in meeting this expectation.

❖ CITING 101

When you submit work with your name on it, the instructor assumes that all of the included words and ideas are yours unless told otherwise. If you do draw on other sources in any way, you are expected to "cite" (identify) those sources. This flags your instructor to which aspects of your paper were drawn from the work of others and provides credit to those sources.

If you fail to properly indicate your sources, it is considered "plagiarism"—taking improper credit for someone else's work. Many students think of plagiarism as submitting entire papers that are blatantly taken from elsewhere, and some students are offended when they are accused of plagiarism on a paper that they have taken hours to write. Contrary to popular belief, though, a plagiarism offense can be as subtle as drawing a sentence or two from another source without using quotation marks, or failing to indicate where a particular fact or idea was obtained. Plagiarism also need not be intentional to be considered plagiarism.

The need to cite sources is typically outlined somewhere in a school's code of conduct or other academic policies. Since the burden rests on students to understand and abide by their school's policies, and plagiarism (intentional or not) can carry serious penalties, feeling comfortable with citation expectations is perhaps one of the most important "gifts" that you can give yourself as a student. It may help to know that your school maintains these expectations for your benefit. Instructors can more clearly assess your writing abilities and your understanding of course content when they know which components of your work were drawn from elsewhere, and which were original to you. This enables them to maintain fair grading practices and defend the integrity of the degree that you are working so hard to earn.

Fairness

You are likely to spend a good deal of time on written assignments. The writing process can be rewarding, but it is also time-consuming and occasionally stressful. It would be understandably infuriating if you spent hours laboring over a paper, only to find out that a classmate had received a higher grade by cutting and pasting sections from the Internet, or by simply rewording the work of another author and submitting it as his or her own. In order to avoid this kind of unfairness, schools maintain a high expectation for students to indicate exactly which elements of their work are attributable to others, and instructors often have solid mechanisms in place to monitor for, and follow up on, plagiarism violations. Some schools will utilize electronic tools, such as Turnitin.com or Blackboard's SafeAssign, to help with the detection of plagiarism.

Institutional Integrity

College degrees are valued for a reason—they signify to potential employers the learning that took place, and the education and training that had been received, during the college experience. Your school's

Figure 9.1   Turnitin.com Originality Report

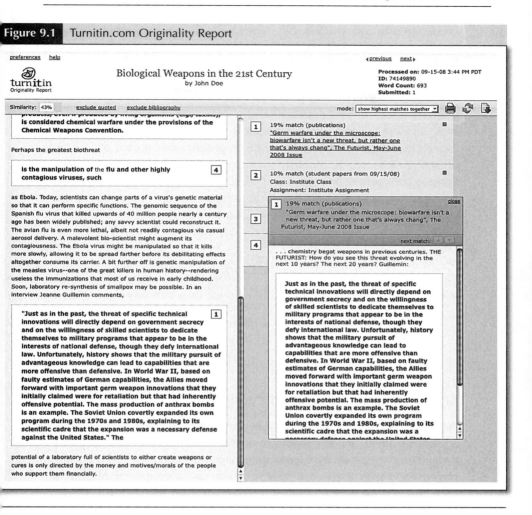

Source: iParadigms, LLC.

plagiarism policy is, in part, an effort to maintain the respectability of your degree. The fairest mechanism for maintaining the integrity of the degree is to hold everyone to the same standard of always clearly demarcating where they have drawn from the work of others, regardless of the magnitude of influence the other work has had.

It Isn't So Bad

The good news is that it is not nearly as complicated as some students fear to appropriately cite sources, and to therefore avoid the potential ramifications of a plagiarism violation. When instructors describe the expectation to cite sources, they typically focus on two aspects: first, the need to give credit where credit is due, a matter that is usually regulated by the school's academic integrity policy; and second, the *format* in which that credit is expected to be given. Instructors sometimes fail to clearly distinguish between these two aspects, which can leave students feeling overwhelmed; the first expectation can carry serious consequences if not met, and the second one entails great detail. Instead of tackling both aspects of citations at once, it may be helpful to first become comfortable with what it means to properly give credit, and then to turn attention to various conventions of formatting. Finally, tips will be provided to assist with preparing to cite sources as you perform research for your papers (a process outlined in greater detail in Chapter 8).

❖ KNOWING *WHEN* TO CITE

While writing papers, you need to provide citations any time that you

- Draw ideas or facts from other sources, even when paraphrased or placed entirely into your own words
- Use the exact words of another in your work

Giving Credit for Ideas and Information

Any time that facts or ideas are taken from other sources, those sources should be given credit. Students are sometimes confused as to why they would need to give credit to a source when they have placed information into their own words. There are a couple of reasons for this. First, citing sources makes it easier for your instructor to provide meaningful feedback on the research that you have done. There is an incredible amount of information readily available to people in the present day; part of what all students should acquire as part of their education, regardless of their school or their field of study, is the ability to differentiate reliable sources from those that contain heavily biased or potentially inaccurate information. Instructors will be looking at the types of sources that you used in your paper.

> Example: If a student makes the bold claim that "smoking doesn't cause cancer" in a paper, the instructor will want to know whether the information was received from a controlled study performed by experienced researchers whose work passed through the rigorous review process of a medical journal, or whether it was information from a recent conversation with a young nephew who just took up the habit.

The second reason to cite the sources of ideas and information is to provide others with credit where it is deserved. Scholars, researchers, and other authors may put years into conducting research for a single publication. Even when you place the information that you have learned into your own words, using others' ideas or conclusions in your paper without giving them credit is still considered plagiarism. Think of it this way: If you had a ground-breaking idea at work, and your boss started to share your idea with high-level corporate decision-makers without giving you credit, you would likely be upset, regardless of whether your boss used your exact words in pitching the idea. Just as you wouldn't want someone else taking credit for your ideas or hard work, you should always give appropriate credit to others in your own writing.

> Learning Tip: Cite the sources of information that you use in your paper, even if you have placed the information into your own words.

Giving Credit for Exact Words

It is also vital to clearly indicate where you have taken exact wording from other sources. It is assumed by your instructor that any wording that appears in your paper is your own, unless otherwise indicated; the use of quotation marks is your way of flagging to your instructor that you have taken those words from elsewhere. Any time that you use wording from another source—even if it is just a short phrase—those words *must* be placed in quotation marks. If you find yourself needing to look back and forth to your source to make sure that you "get the wording right," or if you have cut-and-pasted any number of words from the source, it is good indication that quotation marks are needed. In rare instances certain reference styles will allow some other manner of giving credit for exact wording—for example, APA format allows writers to indent long quotes to indicate that the words are drawn from elsewhere—but when in doubt, use quotation marks.

It is a good idea to limit your use of quotations (the exact words of others) unless the assignment specifically requests otherwise. The instructor is likely looking to assess *your* understanding of the relevant material, and the more your paper is made up of direct quotes, the more difficult it becomes to do so. This author once received a five-page paper from a student that was literally one long quote. While technically the student had not committed an act of plagiarism because the information was properly cited and placed in quotation marks, the student still received a failing grade because it was impossible to properly assess his understanding of the material at hand.

> *Learning Tip: When you take any wording from another source—even a short phrase—place it in quotation marks to give proper credit.*

The Art of Paraphrasing

One mechanism for integrating information from other sources is to put it into your own words—a practice known as "paraphrasing." Done correctly, paraphrased information is presented in an original way that facilitates its flow with the rest of your paper, but it is still followed by a citation to give credit to the source(s) of information. Some students make the mistake of simply changing around just a couple of words in each sentence in their effort to paraphrase, but making such minor changes to the work of another is not enough to truly "make it your own." Since phrases as short as a handful of words still warrant quotation marks, following the original source too closely may still be considered plagiarism. For example, a student may encounter the following statement in her research:

> Frequent hand-washing is one mechanism for preventing the spread of viruses.

She may then state in her work, believing that she does not need quotation marks:

> Hand-washing is one strategy for preventing the spread of illness.

While some words have been changed, the work isn't truly the student's own. When such minor changes are made, the closer approximation of a proper citation might be as follows, with the brackets indicating a minor change in wording that does not alter its meaning, and the ellipses (. . .) indicating the removal of words:

> ". . . hand-washing is one [strategy] for preventing the spread of [illness]."

If properly cited, changing just a couple of words unnecessarily disrupts the flow of the sentence, and changing just a few words is not enough to render quotation marks unnecessary. It is better to commit to quoting the entire sentence directly and using quotation marks if you feel that the author states something in such a poignant manner that it is absolutely essential to your paper that it be included "just so," or to more fully state the information in what are truly your own words—still, of course, indicating the source of the information.

❖ KNOWING *HOW* TO CITE

Giving credit where credit is due will go a long way in meeting expectations, but there is another issue at hand—how, exactly, to do so. Most instructors will hold an expectation that you cite sources in a particular citation style, such as APA or MLA. While you don't need to get all of the stylistic details right to avoid plagiarism charges, instructors may tie some credit to the formatting of your citations. Students should welcome this type of structured guidance; left to their own devices, giving credit to a particular source for an idea could look quite messy. For example, a student might write the following:

> According to what Anne Campbell wrote, back in 1987 in an article that was published in volume 34 issue 5 of a journal called *Social Problems,* female gang members put others down as part of creating their own self image. The article was called "Self Definition by Rejection: The Case of Gang Girls."

The above statement includes all of the information technically needed to give credit to the source, but it isn't very "readable"—the citation information overwhelms the content being shared.

In order to help students and other writers give credit to sources in a more streamlined, "readable" way, a number of organizations have developed rules to standardize the formatting of citations. Conforming to a uniform style helps to ensure that you are including all necessary components in your citations, while simultaneously supporting the readability of your paper. Common citation styles include APA, MLA, and Chicago Style. Different schools and disciplines, and sometimes individual instructors, will have a preference for different citation styles. You can think of these different styles in the same way that you might think of different models of cars—all have the same basic components, but each one will have slightly different features and appearances compared to the others.

Each citation style varies in detail, but in general they each utilize this two-part process of providing a brief in-text citation and a corresponding footnote, endnote, or reference list entry to provide the reader with more information. This allows clear communication of which information was garnered from where without muddling the text of your paper with citation information. Limiting the citation details that you provide in the text of the paper allows your instructor or other readers to focus on the content of your writing, while providing more in-depth reference information elsewhere within your document still enables your instructor to assess the quality of your research. Using APA format as an example, the information about gangs provided above could now read as follows:

> One study indicated that female gang members put others down as part of building their own self-image (Campbell, 1987).

Your instructor could then turn to your reference list entry for more information on the source:

> Campbell, A. (1987). Self-definition by rejection: The case of gang girls. *Social Problems, 34*(5), 451–465.

You can find this practice within any one of your textbooks; if you open them, you are likely to see either in-text citations—e.g., "(Smith, 2006)"—or small numbers that refer the reader to endnotes or footnotes for more information regarding the source(s) of the included information. There is a chance that you haven't even noticed these citations as you have completed your reading assignments; they are there if you need to look up more information on a particular topic or if you are curious regarding the source of a particular fact or idea, but the formatting prevents the disruption of the flow of the text.

In order to facilitate a polished presentation of sources, stylistic guidelines dictate matters down to the smallest detail, such as where to place punctuation, whether to use the word "and" or the symbol "&," and in which order to include different components of information in reference list entries. One of the most intimidating aspects of citing sources can be the level of detail inherent to following a given citation style. Luckily, the organizations that set forth the rules for different styles publish manuals to support students in how to cite different types of sources, and they typically provide examples as well. Once you have tackled proper citations for an assignment or two, it also becomes possible to turn to your own past work for examples this practice minimizes the time that you would otherwise spend looking up the guidelines for various types of resources each time you encounter them.

Figure 9.2	Common Citation Styles		
Citation Style	**Source of Guidelines**	**Example of Full Reference List Entry**	**Example of In-Text Citation**
American Psychological Association (APA)	*Publication Manual of the American Psychological Association*	Suliman, W. A. (2009). Leadership styles of nurse managers in a multinational environment. *Nursing Administration Quarterly, 33*(4), 301–309.	(Suliman, 2009)
Modern Language Association (MLA)	*MLA Handbook for Writers of Research Papers*, or *MLA Style Manual and Guide to Scholarly Publishing*	Suliman, Wafika A. "Leadership Styles of Nurse Managers in a Multinational Environment." *Nursing Administration Quarterly* 33.4 (2009): 301–309. Print.	(Suliman 303)
"Chicago Style" (Established by the University of Chicago Press)	*Chicago Manual of Style*	Suliman, Wafika A. 2009. Leadership styles of nurse managers in a multinational environment. *Nursing Administration Quarterly* 33: 301–309.	(Suliman 2009, 303)

Learning Tip: When citing sources, use the citation style required by your instructor.

❖ PREPARING TO CITE YOUR SOURCES

Some students may find that they are their own worst enemy in trying to properly cite sources. After taking notes from many different books, articles, and Web sites, they may sit down to begin to write, only to find that they have failed to keep a good record of where they have obtained which information. If working from notes, it is nearly impossible to properly indicate the author, year, and page number of a particular quotation unless you kept track of that information while note-taking. Additionally, students may fail to indicate within their own notes when they have written down the exact words from a source, which may lead to inadvertently incorporating the words of other authors into their paper without giving proper credit. Since it is the student's obligation to ensure that sources are appropriately cited, it is crucial to develop a system that allows you to consistently keep track of which information you have received from which source. Some possible organizational systems are as follows:

- *If you often find yourself relying too heavily on the words of others,* use a different index card for each source. Write the citation information for the source on one side—author, year, title, etc.—and take notes on the other. Use the limited space as incentive to summarize what you have learned in your own words. If you do find an exact quote that is particularly poignant, though, you can still record it—simply be sure to place it in quotation marks and to take note of the page number.

- *If you are using hard-copy sources,* or can print sources that you have found online, you can highlight quotes that you may want to integrate into your paper, and summarize the information that you learn in the margins of that source. That way, as you integrate information, you know exactly which source to cite.

- *If you prefer to organize your notes by theme rather than by source,* assign a number (1, 2, 3, etc.) or letter (A, B, C, etc.) to each source. As you take notes on different themes that you find in a number of different sources, this provides a quick way of you indicating to yourself where you had received which information. As you take notes, be sure to place any exact wording that you copy into quotation marks.

- *If you prefer to do most of your work on the computer,* you can create a separate word processing document for notes from each of your sources. At the top of each document, include the information that you would need to reference that source. If you might use the source for more than one paper, you can even save yourself time in the future by placing the reference information in the proper format for ultimate inclusion in your reference list/works cited, so that you can simply cut and paste that information each time you write a paper instead of laboring over the proper formatting each time that you use the source in a paper.

❖ CONCLUSION

It is your responsibility to consistently "give credit where credit is due" in your schoolwork. You will need to clearly indicate to the instructor

Figure 9.3   Example of Comprehensive Notes

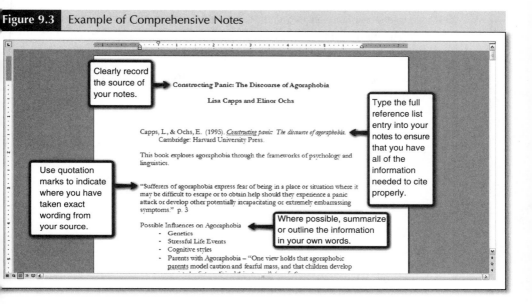

which wording, ideas, or information were gathered from other sources by providing quotation marks, in-text citations, and a reference list (or footnotes/endnotes). While the level of detail regulated by most citation styles can seem intimidating at first, taking the time to learn how to cite properly will benefit you throughout your schooling and beyond.

REFLECTION QUESTIONS

1. Why is it important to cite your sources even if you have placed information into your own words?

2. What are some benefits of conforming to a certain citation style when you cite your sources?

3. Does the method that you use for taking notes on your research facilitate your ability to properly give credit where credit is due? How might you improve your current note-taking methods?

CHAPTER CHECKLIST

☐ Look up and read your school's plagiarism/academic honesty policy.

☐ Find out whether your instructor (or school) requires a certain citation style in your writing.

☐ If a certain citation style is required of you, locate appropriate resources, such as a Web site or publication manual, that will support you in properly formatting your citations.

☐ Compose a document with sample in-text citations and reference list entries for you own future reference. Include sample citations of journal articles, Web sites, and books.

RELATED RESOURCES

APA and MLA, General Writing	http://owl.english.purdue.edu
APA	www.apastyle.org
MLA	www.mla.org/style
Citation Tool	www.calvin.edu/library/knightcite/index.php
Citation Tool	www.easybib.com
Citation Tool	http://citationmachine.net
Plagiarism Detection	www.turnitin.com

Index

"Abstract conceptualization"
    learning style, 78–79
Academic catalog, 46
Academic journals, 102–103, 105, 106
Academic research vs. personal
    beliefs, 96–97
Academic support, 49–51, 58
Accommodators, 78–79
"Active experimentation" learning
    style, 78–79
Administrators, 70–71
Advisors, 46
Allocation of time, 38–42
American Psychological Association
    (APA) format, 114, 115, 118
Announcements, 22–23
Anti-virus programs, 17
APA (American Psychological
    Association) format, 114, 115, 118
Assignment submission, 22–23,
    26–27
Assimilators, 78–80
Asynchronous component, 25
Attendance, 24–25
Auditory learners, 75, 77, 81
Automatic "save" settings, 63–64

Backup of electronic files, 63–65, 72
Balance in life, 29, 41–42
Benefits of online education, 2, 6–7
Bias in research sources, 99, 101
Blended courses, 24–25
Books as research sources, 102,
    103–105, 106
Bookstores, online, 102, 103, 105, 106
Brainstorming work spaces, 33

Breaks in work, 40
Broadband Internet connection,
    17–18
Businesses providing technical
    support, 47–48

Calendar for deadlines, 10
Carpools, 40
Cellular connection to Internet, 18
Challenges
    family/personal emergencies, 68–69
    mental illness, 52, 54, 58
    online participation while
        incapacitated, 90
    physical limitations, 69–70
    school conflicts, 70–71
Chicago style, 115
Childcare, 40–41
Citation of sources
    examples, 115, 117
    preparation for, 115–116
    reasons for, 107–110
    styles, 113–115, 117–118
    when to provide, 90–91, 110–113
Classroom platforms, 20–21
Comfort of work spaces, 36
Communication
    discussion boards, 25, 65,
        66, 84–91
    e-mail, 23, 91–92
    misunderstandings, 84
    traditional classrooms, 83–84
    when crises occur, 68–71
    See also Social networks; Writing
Computers
    access, 16

malfunctions, 47–48, 67
software, 18–19, 28
tutorials, 4, 5, 13
Web sites for support, 58
See also Technology
Computer-to-computer calling
services, 52, 59
"Concrete experience" learning
style, 78–79
Confrontations, avoiding, 87–88
Convergers, 78–80
Counseling services, 52, 54
Crises. *See* Challenges

Data recovery, 48
Deadlines, 9–10, 22–23, 25–27, 71
Dial-up Internet, 17
Directions, following, 85
Disappointment at "settling," 2
Discussion boards, 25, 65, 66, 84–91
Document recovery settings, 63–64
"Doing" learning style, 78–80

E-books, 105, 106
Educational institutions'
Web sites, 101
Electronic books, 105, 106
Electronic files, 31–32, 63–65, 72
E-mail, 23, 91–92
Emergencies. *See* Challenges
Emoticons, 88, 91, 94
Emotions
apprehension, 3
crises bringing on, 68–69
disappointment at "settling," 2
loneliness, 4–5
stress-related, 61–62
technology-induced, 3–4, 7,
62–63, 65–66
Employment
rules for using resources, 33
statistics, 68
time management and, 40
work emergencies, 68–69
Encyclopedias, 101
Enrollment statistics, x, 4
Environments for study.
See Work spaces
Error messages, 48
Etiquette, online, 88, 91, 94

Expectations of instructors,
85, 107–108
Exploration of virtual spaces, 19–22
External academic support, 50–51

Facebook, 52, 53, 59
FAFSA, 54–55
Familiarity with online
environments, 7
Family emergencies, 68–69
Family support, 6
Feelings. *See* Emotions
Finances, household, 56–57
Financial aid, 54–56, 58
Flashcards, 50
Formal writing assignments, 93

Gardner, Howard, 74–75
Government Web sites, 100–101
Gradable elements, 24
Graduation requirements, 46–47
Grants, 55

"Hands-on" labs, 77
Help
academic resources, 49–51
misconceptions about, 45–46
school-specific resources, 46–47
social resources, 51–52
technology resources, 47–49
Hotlines, counseling, 54
Household finances, 56–57
Household patterns, 37
"House rules," 6, 7
Hybrid courses, 24–25

Illness/injury
deadlines affected by, 90
mental disturbances, 52, 54, 58
physical limitations, 69–70
Income, increasing, 57
Industry Web sites, 102
Injuries. *See* Illness/injury
Instant messaging tools, 51–52
Institutional integrity, 108–109
Instructors
contacting, 5, 49, 77
expectations of, 85, 107–108
involving in conflict
management, 70–71

Intelligences, multiple, 74–75
Internet connections
    cellular phones, 18
    dial-up vs. broadband, 17–18
    in public work spaces, 37–38
    troubleshooting, 48, 66
    voice/video calls, 52, 59
    wireless networks, 35–36, 37–38
    See also Web sites
Interpersonal intelligence, 74–75

Journal articles, 102–103, 105, 106

Kinesthetic learners, 76, 77
Kolb, David, 77–80

Learning styles
    knowing yourself, 73–74, 80–81
    Kolb's theories, 77–80
    multiple intelligences, 74–75
    sensory preferences, 75
Library resources, 50, 104, 105
Loans, 55
Local business support, 47–48
Loneliness, 4–5

Manual backups, 65
Mass media (traditional), 99–100,
    103, 106
Mass transit, 40
Math centers, 49–50
Mental illness, 52, 54, 58
Mentors/study buddies, 49
Misinformation on Web sites,
    100–102
MLA (Modern Language
    Association) format, 115, 118
Mobile broadband connection, 18
Modern Language Association
    (MLA) format, 115, 118
Multiple intelligences, 74–75
Myths about online learning, 1–12

Naps, 39, 42
News stories, 99–100
Nonfiction books, 102, 103, 106

Office space, 30–31, 37–38
Off-topic discussions, 86–87
One-on-one assistance, 49

Online etiquette, 88, 91, 94
On-the-road study pack, 31
On-topic, staying, 86–87
Opinion vs. academic research, 96–97
Organizational skills, 30–32, 93
Organization of citations, 115–116
Organizations' Web sites, 101

Paraphrasing, 110–111, 112–113
Parenting time, 40–41
Peer-reviewed journals, 103
Perseverance, 61–62
Personal beliefs vs. academic
    research, 96–97
Personal experiences in research
    papers, 98–99
Personal support resources, 58
Perspective, maintaining, 61–62
Physical limitations/illness,
    69–70, 90
Plagiarism, 90–91, 108–109, 118
Platforms, classroom, 20–21
Podcasts, 77
Portals, 20
Postings. *See* Discussion boards
Process of becoming an e-learner, x–xi
Productivity, 35
Professionalism, 91–92
Professors. *See* Instructors
Programs, software, 18–19
Publicly available resources,
    51–52, 53, 54
Public study locations, 37–38

Quotation marks, 111–113

"Real-world" learners, 77
"Reflective observation" learning
    style, 78–79
Requirements for graduation, 46–47
Research
    citations used to evaluate, 110
    importance of, 96
    opinion vs., 96–97
    types of resources for, 97–103
    See also specific resource
Ride shares, 40

Schedules for studying, 39–42
Scholarly articles, 102–103, 105, 106

Scholarly books, 102, 103, 106
Scholarships, 55
School-based resources
    libraries, 50, 104, 105
    mentors/study buddies, 49
    social networks, 51
    technical support, 47
    writing/math centers, 49–50
School-related problems, 70–71
Self-checking, 86–87
Self-paced education, myth of, 9–10
Sensory preferences, 75–77
Sleep, 39, 42
Socializing, 86
Social networks, 50, 51–52, 53, 59
Software, 18–19, 28
Space requirements at home, 36
Spell check features, 89–90, 91
Spending reductions, 56
Stigmatization, 11
Stress, 61–62
Student networks, 6
"Study dates," 50
Study materials online, 50–51
Study packs, on-the-road, 31
Study tips (Web sites for), 43, 81
Styles, citation, 113–115, 117–118
Submission of assignments,
    22–23, 26–27
Syllabus, 22
Synchronous components, 24–25

Tactile learners, 76, 77
Technology
    delivery tools, 11–12
    discussion boards, 25, 65, 66, 84–91
    electronic files, 31–32, 63–65, 72
    experience online, 7
    feelings about, 3–4, 7, 62–63, 65–66
    software, 18–19
    support for, 19, 47–49, 58, 67
    virus protection, 17
    See also Computers; Internet
        connections
Telephone services, 18, 52, 59
"Text talk," 88–89
"Thinking" learning style, 78–80
Time management, 8–9, 38–42, 43
Traditional education, 11
Traditional mass media,
    99–100, 103, 106

Transition to online education, 3
Transportation time, 40
Tuition reimbursement, 56
Turnitin.com, 108, 109, 118
Tutorials, 4, 5, 13
Tutors, 49

University of Chicago Press style, 115

Veterans, funding for, 56
Virus protection, 17
Visual learners, 75, 76, 81
"Voice over Internet Protocol"
    (VoIP) services, 52, 59
Voice recognition software, 70, 72

Waiting time, using, 39–40
"Watching" learning style, 78–80
Web sites
    academic support, 58
    auditory learners, 81
    computer/software companies,
        28, 48, 58
    financial aid, 54–55, 58
    library resources, 104, 105
    misinformation on, 100–102
    multiple intelligences, 75
    online etiquette, 94
    personal support, 58
    plagiarism, 108, 109, 118
    research tools, 100–102, 106
    social tools, 59
    study tips, 43, 81
    time management, 43
    tutorials, 13
    visual learners, 81
    voice recognition software, 72
    writing resources, 60, 94, 118
Wi-fi connections, 35–36
Wikipedia, 101
Wireless Internet connections,
    35–36, 37–38
Word processing backups, 63–65, 72
Work spaces, 32–38, 43
Writing
    formal assignments, 93
    handling physical limitations,
        69–70
    resources, 49–50, 51, 60, 93, 94
    See also Citation of sources;
        Communication

About the Author

Julie L. Globokar holds a master's degree and is currently pursuing her PhD in criminal justice from the University of Illinois at Chicago. She has extensive experience with both online and face-to-face instruction at the college level, and she has served for three years as an academic chair for online courses in Kaplan University's Undergraduate School of Criminal Justice. She is dedicated to helping students overcome barriers to reach their goals.